AMERICAN INDIAN SOCIETIES

Cultural Survival Report 32

AMERICAN INDIAN SOCIETIES
Strategies and Conditions of
Political and Cultural Survival

Duane Champagne

Cultural Survival, Inc.
Cambridge, Massachusetts

Cultural Survival, Inc.
11 Divinity Avenue
Cambridge, MA 02138
(617) 495-2562

Printed in the United States of America
by Transcript Printing Company, Peterborough, NH 03458

Cultural Survival Report 32
The Cultural Survival Report is a continuation of the Occasional Paper series.

Library of Congress Cataloging-in-Publication Data
Champagne, Duane.
    American Indian Societies : strategies and conditions of political and
cultural survival / Duane Champagne.
        p.   cm. — (Cultural survival report : 32)
    Includes bibliographical references.
    ISBN 0-939521-46-6 : $19.95. — ISBN 0-939521-43-1 : (pbk.) $10.00.
    1. Indians of North America — Government relations.   2. Indians of North
America — Social life and customs.   3. Indians of North America — Cultural
assimilation.   I. Title.   II. Series.
    E91.C455 1989
    306'.08997 — dc20   89-17157
                                                                                CIP

Preface

Many cultures throughout the world have been and are now confronted by issues similar to those encountered by American Indian societies over the past 400 years. By examining the similarities and differences in societal differentiation, cultural world views, and institutions of social and political solidarity among several American Indian societies, as well as examining historical relations of geopolitical competition, world-system incorporation, and the interpenetration of cultural and normative ideals from colonizing nations and state, I present an historical and comparative method for explaining the empirical range of change within social and political organization as institutional responses for ensuring political and cultural survival. With appropriate consideration for differences in geopolitical environment, world-system locality, and institutional order, this analysis should be applicable to the study of social and political change in indigenous societies in other parts of the world and in other historical periods. Such an analysis would seek to identify the specific institutional and/or external conditions and supports that indigenous societies, who face colonizing powers, may need to retain political and cultural autonomy.

Acknowledgments

Research and writing support for this report came from the Rockefeller Foundation, the Ford Foundation, a faculty Senate Grant from UCLA, the American Indian Studies Center at UCLA, and the National Science Foundation (Grant No. SES-853914). Thanks also goes to Cultural Survival for administering the Rockefeller Foundation award. I gratefully acknowledge permission from the Newberry Library to reprint portions of "American

Bureaucratization and Tribal Governments: Problems of Institutionalization at the Community Level" (in *Occasional Papers in Curriculum Series* Number 5. Chicago: Newberry Library, 1987). I also gratefully acknowledge permission from the Tlingit-Haida Central Council to quote from *The Central Council 50 Years* by Peter Metcalfe (Juneau, AK: The Council of the Tlingit & Haida Indians of Alaska, 1985).

Contents

Chapter 1

Introduction

IN ONE WAY OR ANOTHER, American Indians have resisted the political and cultural intrusions of colonizing Western societies. Although their primary purpose has been to maintain control over territory and to preserve political and cultural autonomy, the ways in which these societies have responded to Western contact vary considerably: revitalization movements, cultural traditionalism, passive resistance, state formation, secular political movements, and political-social fragmentation. Why are these responses so varied? Do they reveal a pattern?

A simple evolutionary approach to the study of Native American responses to Western contact can explain little. For example, the assumption that Native American societies are largely defined by hunter-gatherer or horticultural economic organization leaves little reason to believe that they will respond differently to similar conditions of Western contact. Other descriptions of "primitive" social organization describe Native American societies as acephalous, segmentary, or lacking in political centralization or political unity; however, even these categorizations are blunt instruments for analyzing the variation in the social order of Native American societies and their different responses to Western contact. Describing some Native American societies as tribal societies or as chiefdoms and others as acephalous tends to discount the considerable differences in cultural, political, and social organization in native North America.

For example, the Tlingit of the southern panhandle of present Alaska were a hunting, fishing, and gathering society with an elaborate material culture but no national political leaders or centralized political institutions. The

Natchez of present-day Louisiana had a horticultural and hunting society that was politically and ceremonially centralized. The French destroyed the Natchez in 1730; the Tlingit continue to survive and practice their culture, and have adopted new forms of democratic political organization and corporate and small-scale business management. Thus historical events play a central role in the survival of any particular group; to merely classify a society's economic or social organization is not an infallible predictor of its survival or of the way it will respond to Western impacts. Native American societies are culturally and institutionally complex, and vary considerably in cultural, social, and political organization. This variation provides a major key to understanding the different changes in Native American societies. In order to understand these variations, we should first observe their institutional orders and then study their changes over the historical events of contact with Western economic, political, and cultural institutions.

Collective Action and Social Change

Collective action takes place when a group acts to pursue a common interest (Tilly 1978:7), such as when political parties try to gain control over or access to the government. Whenever a group attempts to gain some political or economic advantage but is not changing societal rules, it is engaged in routine conflict, generally the struggle over control resources (wealth, political power, status). Such group action does not challenge the fundamental rules of political or normative organization, but attempts to secure advantages within the legitimately defined institutional order. An example of routine conflict can be seen in sporting events, where one must have physical force and competitive drive to win a football game, but must also obey the rules in order for the opponents and spectators to recognize the victory.

Another example more salient to this book is the collective action that took place at Custer's Last Stand. In this brief military encounter, Custer and his men, and the Sioux and their Cheyenne allies, were engaged in collective military action and goals. On both sides, most participating social actors adhered to the demands of their social, political, cultural, and military institutions. None of them tried to change their own societies; in fact, each conformed to their societies' normative, cultural, and political demands despite the fact that to engage in battle could mean individual death. These events did not directly or intentionally lead to social change in Cheyenne or Sioux societies. Collective actions, such as military expeditions or defenses, are not necessarily central events for understanding processes of social change; they usually occur within a nation's preexisting military institutional order, and are not intended to change the fundamental organization of the society (although losing the battle or war can have great consequences for the future and organization of the society).

When an indigenous society is confronted by a colonial power or powers, it can respond by changing its institutional order (i.e., by centralizing and secularizing political power and institutions or by accepting economic innovations) or it can adhere to its preexisting institutional order. If a society refuses or is unable to change its institutional order despite pressing changes in its economic and political environment, such a response is often called traditionalistic. A society might prefer to retain the central feature of its social and culture order, and respond to changing economic and political conditions with collective action that conforms to its preexisting societal order. If such a society was able to retain its territory and its cultural and national identities, then we would certainly want to know what aspects of its institutions enabled it to withstand colonial pressures.

Not all collective or social actions are categorized as routine conflict; some seek to secure changes in the cultural, political, normative, or economic order of the society. Since this book focuses on issues of societal response and change, social and collective movements that lead to institutionalized change in the social order are of more importance here. The term *social change* can be defined as the institutionalization of increased specialization of relations among cultural, normative, political, and economic institutions, and increased specialization of the rules of cultural order, normative order, political organization, and economic organization. Social change is not an automatic or evolutionary process; concrete groups must introduce innovations and gain the economic, political, and social support necessary for the innovation to endure (Parsons 1977; Eisenstadt 1978:25–34). Whenever an institutional innovation (e.g., the establishment of a centralized political structure where there was none before) gains cultural legitimacy, political and social support, and sufficient economic resources, then that new institution is consensually institutionalized. When innovators cannot gain social or political support or secure symbolic legitimacy, they might use force, through political or military power, to impose their views on the remaining members of the society. Although such an innovation is coercively institutionalized and is often considered inherently unstable, many coercive regimes have endured for long historical periods.

Institutionalized change is the main concern here; innovations and changes that do not become institutionalized have little effect on a society or its future. For example, although the Ghost Dance practiced in the early 1890s among numerous Indian plains nations has received considerable press, the movement failed to become an institutionalized part of all but a very few plains societies, and is thus of little interest in the study of social change. The less dramatic peyote religion, which the plains societies practiced during the second half of the nineteenth century, was an alternative that has been significantly more enduring and has become a regular feature of the culture of many contemporary reservation communities. Consequently, the peyote cult is of much greater significance for understanding societal change than the more dramatic Ghost Dance movement.

The literature on native North Americans tends to regard Indian societies as endemic with internal factionalism. However, what many observers have recorded is largely routine conflict. Since many Indian societies are politically decentralized, with segmentary bands, villages, or kinship groups having considerable local political, social, and economic autonomy, they have considerable difficulty organizing sustained collective action; each major subgroup has the right to make most of its own decisions on whether to participate with other groups or to follow a different strategy. While such absence of concerted action may look like factionalism, the major subgroups are merely exercising their prerogative to make their own political decisions. Such conflict must be considered routine conflict because it conforms to existing rules of the social and political order.

The term *factionalism* should be reserved for conflicts over the rules of societal order. When a society breaks into conflicting groups that cannot agree on fundamental rules of social order, then it can be said to be divided into factional cleavages. To some extent factional cleavages occur in all societies, but they are most apparent among Indian societies with respect to the conflicts between "progressives" and traditionals, Christians and pagans — those who prefer to accept varying degrees of social, economic and political innovation as opposed to those who prefer to adhere to the preexisting institutional and cultural order. Factionalism is a different kind of conflict from routine conflict; it often reflects no common ground, and therefore leads to the potential for civil war, violence, or coercive domination by the most powerful groups. A close analogy of institutional conflict is the struggle in contemporary large-scale societies between communists and capitalists. Communists and capitalists hold fundamentally incompatible views of social order; there is little ground for compromise or consensus. The case is similar in Native American societies when missionaries and Christian converts attempt to introduce new cultural and religious world views, or when some groups attempt to impose a centralized, democratic government on a society in which ceremonially integrated but politically decentralized village or kin-based governments have reigned from time immemorial.

Geopolitical Environment, World System, and Cultural Interpenetration

Colonial contact is a powerful source of change in indigenous societies, so powerful that many analysts tend to consider the conditions of contact determinant and do not systematically analyze the social and political orders of the indigenous nations. Such a position reduces the response of indigenous societies to mere reflections or reactions to the powerful forces of colonial societies. This view tends to ignore or understate the strategies and choices that indigenous societies make in attempting to cope and survive within a hostile geopolitical environment and competitive world system.

Nevertheless, the forces of contact are powerful and major instigators of change in indigenous societies, and no explanation of variation in institutional response to Western contact can be complete without their due consideration. Here we consider three major forms of contact — geopolitical environment, world system, and cultural-normative interpenetration — and will treat them as if they are analytically independent, meaning that conceptual distinctions can be between any two relations, although in historical, empirical settings they may be interrelated. This leaves open the possibility that one form of contact is not necessarily reducible to one or both of the other dimensions, and that in empirical, historical settings one condition may predominate over the others. This argument may sound straightforward, but it entails certain fundamental assumptions. Geopolitical environment, world-system relations, and cultural-normative interpenetration are considered analytically autonomous levels of analysis. Furthermore, it holds as a hypothesis the Marxist assumption that culture and political order are ultimately reducible to the conditions of the mode of production, or the world system argument that political order and culture are of secondary importance to location within the world system for determining the organization and characteristics of political order in peripheral societies (Engels 1972; Wallerstein 1984:3–58).

Geopolitical environment can be defined in terms of competition, hegemony, and direct administrative domination. A competitive geopolitical environment occurs when two or more colonial powers contend for political and economic control over territory occupied by several indigenous societies. In North American history, the period between 1600 and 1795 (except for the 1760-to-1777 period of British hegemony) is characterized by competition between several European imperial powers struggling to control the fur trade and territory in eastern North America. Hegemonic political conditions are obtained when one colonial power establishes a sphere of influence over a region and does not encounter significant political or trade competition from rival imperial powers. In American history, the period between 1795 and 1890 – with few exceptions, such as the Civil War and the War of 1812 – can be characterized as a hegemonic situation. During most of this period, American Indian societies retained considerable rights of self-government, but the increasingly powerful US political and economic expansion threatened and ultimately greatly impaired their political autonomy and territorial rights.

Administrative domination occurs when the colonizing power has direct political control over the land, resources, and institutions of the indigenous societies. For most Native American societies, administrative subordination began when they were restricted to a reservation. By the 1890s, most federally recognized American Indian societies were forced or induced to live on reservations – usually small remnants of their original lands. For the next several decades, a period known for its assimilationist Indian policy, US government agencies – primarily the Office of Indian Affairs – deliberately tried to eradicate Indian governments and culture while pursuing a policy of turning Indians into US citizens through education and agricultural training. The late 1920s saw several reports that exposed the failure of these policies, and in 1934 the Wheeler-Howard Act ushered in the Indian New Deal, which allowed tribes to organize governments and extend more control over reservation economic resources. The late forties brought a turnabout with the introduction of the termination policy, a policy designed to abolish Indian reservations and incorporate Indians into US society. By the early sixties, Indian protests, lobbying, and reluctant states curtailed the termination policy. The current period is called *self-determination*. Despite attempts in recent years to allow tribal governments more cultural and political autonomy, the US government, through the Department of the Interior and the Bureau of Indian Affairs (BIA), continues to exercise considerable administrative control over reservation institutions, land, and resources, as well as veto power over many reservation government decisions (Taylor 1984; Castile 1974; Garbarino 1980; Champagne 1983a, Jorgensen 1986).

Most indigenous societies within the United States came under federal administrative domination, although important exceptions do exist. In the southwest, the indigenous nations of present-day New Mexico, southern California, Texas, and Arizona were under Spanish colonial administration from the late 1500s to the early 1800s, and then under Mexican administration after the Mexican Revolution until US annexation in the late 1840s and 1850s (Hall 1989). The southwest was always a peripheral area for both the Spanish and Mexican governments, although their methods of economic, political and cultural incorporation resemble the colonial conditions of Central and South America much more than they do the eastern and northern United States and Canada. The Spanish ruled through direct military conquest and administrative domination for purposes of economic exploitation. The indigenous nations in the Spanish-dominated colonies, with the exception of those in West Florida and Florida, did not experience the sequence of competitive, rival imperial powers that characterizes much of the colonial history of North America from about 1600 to the end of the War of 1812. Most native North American societies retained political independence for several centuries after Western contact, and were not subject to the large-scale conquests that characterized the Spanish conquest after the early 1500s. The more competitive political conditions outside of the areas of Spanish conquest allowed greater possibilities for institutional change as a strategy for territorial and national survival.

A second major exception to US bureaucratic domination was the absence of strong administrative controls over the native Alaskan societies. Although Alaska was a Russian colony, and the Russian colonial period devastated the economies of some of the Aleutian villages, the Russian population was small and restricted largely to the coastal regions. The more densely populated southern panhandle nations, such as the Tlingit, were never completely subjugated to Russian rule. When the United States purchased Alaska in 1867, it made no provisions for the rights of native societies, and for several decades exercised little administrative authority over them. Alaska's indigenous groups were subject to territorial laws rather than to the oversight of the Office of Indian Affairs. As will be seen further on, the relative absence of BIA administrative control over Alaska native villages, land, and resources was a condition that facilitated the formation of a statewide land claim movement in the late 1960s and early 1970s.

The conditions of geopolitical relations are central to explaining institutional change or collective action. Administrative control or internal colonialism inhibit the chances for subordinated groups to achieve or retain political or cultural autonomy (Wolf 1969:290; Skocpol 1979:115; Tilly 1978:81–84). Hegemonic or competitive situations, in which indigenous societies retain self-government and control over their own institutions and resources, offer more possibilities for concerted collective action and responses involving change in the institutional order (Skocpol 1979:115–117; Tilly 1978:81–84). Nevertheless, geopolitical conditions do not determine the responses of indigenous societies; other factors can have equally compelling effects.

Incorporation into markets or world-system relations is a macro order process, which, like geopolitical environments, is largely beyond the will and control of the members of indigenous societies. Most native North American societies were incorporated into the skin or fur trade sometime during their history. They traded furs for European manufactured goods such as guns, ammunition, metal products, textiles, and, often, whiskey. As the Indians replaced bone and stone tools with guns and hatchets, indigenous craftsmanship gave way to reliance on trade. The fur trade flourished from 1600 to the early 1800s; its subsequent decline occurred as the price for furs fell and American mountain men assumed much of the trade business.

For many Native Americans, the collapse of the fur trade meant economic impoverishment, the sale of land and economic dependence and political subordination on US government reservations. By the late 1870s, the annihilation of the buffalo herds in the Great Plains area had catastrophic effects on the trade and subsistence economies of the plains nations. Some societies were fortunate enough to have access to alternate or new market relations after the decline of the fur trade: the four major southeastern nations — the Cherokee, Choctaw, Chickasaw, and Creek — were incorporated into the southern plantation export market. The requirements of cotton production — large-scale plantations and slave labor in the antebellum South — led to economic stratification and class structures in all four southern societies. Similarly the societies of the Pacific Northwest region, such as the Tlingit, were less affected by the decline of the fur trade because they had retained their subsistence base — in the Tlingit's case, fishing and hunting. Such societies, along with those that accepted alternative markets or subsistence methods acceptable to their skills and cultural orientations, had greater economic resources for mounting sustained collective efforts and for introducing institutional change.

The third major impact, cultural-normative interpenetration, differs from market incorporation and geopolitical relations insofar as it enters the society through changes in the cultural-normative order of a society. Contact with Western traders made members of indigenous societies aware of alternate world views, political organizations, religions, and social mores. Simply having knowledge of Western culture provides little understanding of social change unless it forms the basis for altering the indigenous social order or is taken as a negative model in an effort to preserve the traditional, indigenous social-cultural order. Some members of indigenous societies internalized Western models of cultural, social, political, and economic organization through education, Christian conversion, and life experience. The acceptance or rejection of Western models varies from individual to individual and from society to society. Factional conflict might arise between groups who suggest change based on models of Western institutional order and those who reject such change, depending on the nature of the innovation — does it fundamentally reorganize the cultural or institutional order, or is it considered secondary and therefore acceptable?

These perceptions vary from society to society. The introduction of Christianity into Iroquois society, for example, caused sharp factional cleavages between Christians and non-Christians throughout the nineteenth century. The Cherokee, after some initial disruption, accepted a more pluralistic view, allowing each community to choose its religious persuasion. Similar cleavages can be observed in other societies; the society's institutional order and the character of the innovation are central for determining whether change will be consensually institutionalized or rejected, or will result in violent community splits. Institutional innovations are a precondition for change, but an insufficient one—any particular innovation can fail.

Social Order and Change

Market incorporation, cultural interpenetration, and geopolitical conditions can all influence the responses available to indigenous societies, but more critical in determining the variation in the responses is social-cultural organization. Social change has been defined as a process of institutionalization; to institutionalize an innovation in society—if it is to be permanent or significant—depends on availability of resources and on the innovating group's capacity to gather social, cultural, and political commitments in support of change (Eisenstadt 1964:235–247; Alexander and Colomy 1985:13–16; Smelser 1985:226). Support for any particular innovation depends on the preexisting cultural order and its derivative norms and values, the preexisting level of institutional flexibility (or societal differentiation), and the forms of social and political solidarity.

Social solidarity differs from political solidarity. Almost all societies have institutions, norms, values, or cultural orientations shared by most members. The members of most Native American societies share common world views, norms, values, and ceremonies, and know the rules of political organization and economic subsistence—a kind of social integration that Durkheim called *mechanical solidarity* (Durkheim 1984). Despite these shared understandings, however, in most indigenous societies such social consensus did not translate into sustained or institutionalized national collective political commitments. In order to respond collectively or institutionally to colonial threats, a society must attain a level of collective solidarity that transcends individual, local, or particularistic commitments. Few, if any, native North American societies formed political nationalities before Western contact, and only a handful formed secular political nationalities in the postcontact period. Most Indian societies were politically decentralized; their polities were composed of local villages, bands, or kinship groups that retained considerable local powers of political decision making (Sahlins 1968:20; Lowie 1967:63–68). Some argue that the formation of extralocal institutions in many Native American societies was solely the result of responses to Western contact (Fried 1971); however, this argument is not congruent with the hierarchically organized societies of the pre-Columbian Mississippi Culture (900–1600 A.D.) and those reported in the de Soto manuscripts in the southeast for the period 1538–1542 (Bourne 1922).

One reason that societies with segmentary political organization have difficulty mounting sustained collective action is that leaders of major social or political units make decisions by consensus. Any group that disagrees is not bound to participate in the majority decision. During the contact period, the issues became increasingly complex, resulting in little agreement and hence little collective action. Societies with national institutions of social integration are more likely to reach consensus, mount sustained collective actions, and adopt institutional change. These societies are also more likely to form collective national political orientations; the specific type of response, however, also depends on other features such as the configuration of societal differentiation and cultural orientations.

The concept of institutional flexibility derives from the theory of structural differentiation (Parsons 1977; Smelser 1973; Eisenstadt 1978:64–66). It implies that more differentiated societies (i.e., those with more specialized and autonomous institutions) will have greater capacities to accept and institutionalize change. Here we are concerned primarily with the relations of differentiation among the major macro-level political, economic, cultural, and normative spheres of society. Secondary attention will be given to the internal differentiation or complexity within the political, cultural, economic, and normative institutions. For example, internal differentiation within the economic sphere refers to the specialization within the division of labor, which is often assumed to be simple in indigenous societies and complex in industrial societies. Most differentiation theorists have focused on the division of labor, and have understated the significance of internal differentiation of the polity, or relations between the economy and society, polity, and culture. Expanding the division of labor leads to increased production of surplus value, but the use of such surplus value is determined within the context of the society's cultural, political, and normative organization.

The theory of structural differentiation indicates that certain institutional configurations will facilitate adoption of social change and others will present obstacles. Less differentiated societies have less capacity for institutionalizing change because the overlapping nature of their institutional configurations requires simultaneous change in more than one major societal sector. For example, Northern Cheyenne mythology says that the prophet Sweet Medicine gave the Cheyenne their laws and their government of the Council of 44 Chiefs. In Cheyenne society, the religious sphere defines its political organization, and polity and culture are not differentiated. Well-socialized Cheyennes, therefore, would not voluntarily change their political organization without first securing some form of religious sanction. Political change in a society with nondifferentiated political and cultural orders requires modifications in both spheres (Eisenstadt 1967:444); only under extreme conditions can major changes occur simultaneously in both spheres. The members of societies with little societal differentiation tend to resist institutional innovation; they have little capacity for autonomous group formation and prefer to expend their energies preserving the prevailing institutional order (Eisenstadt 1978:66).

In a more differentiated society — e.g., one in which the polity differs from kinship organization — changes in the political sphere do not require that the kinship groups reorganize or suppress their traditional rights. Therefore, kin groups will not resist a proposed political innovation, because it does not directly change or threaten their prerogatives. Such societies should encounter fewer institutional obstacles to change than those with less differentiated institutional configurations (Eisenstadt 1978:66; Parsons 1977).

Although the theory of differentiation tells us to look to relations of specialization and autonomy among and within the major institutional spheres of society in order to understand the variations in societal change, the theory is nevertheless very general and can only be used as a heuristic device. The theory's evolutionary underpinning is that societies move from less differentiated to more differentiated levels. The method presented in this book differs from this classical reasoning. In order to develop a more empirically grounded argument, the institutional configurations of differentiation will be described and analyzed here within historically contingent settings. The purpose is to use historical analysis to find the major social trends of change and continuity in societies with specific forms of institutional differentiation. This requires classifying societies according to the relations of differentiation, as well as institutions of social and political integration and cultural world view, as a means for understanding the trends of change in societies from one institutional configuration to another, and also to analyze the processes, groups, events, conditions, and resources associated with those changes.

Societies do not necessarily move toward greater societal differentiation; some societies grow less differentiated. Others accept differentiation, but in only one or two major societal spheres — e.g., in political relations with the formation of a state system. The possibilities and trends of change in the differentiation of societies must be left theoretically open until historical analysis can provide greater understanding of the variation in configurations of differentiated institutions, and in their change and continuity in a variety of historical settings. The theory of differentiation merely shows how to classify societies in a certain way; this might help in understanding the possibilities of social change, but it tells us little about the historical processes of change in specific empirical societies.

There is no single Native American culture or normative order; native North America is composed of hundreds of different societies with numerous languages, religious orientations, and world views. Consequently, each society must be analyzed separately for its institutional relations of differentiation, its social and political solidarity, its economic organization, and its cultural-normative order as an interrelated societal order. Subtle differences in societal differentiation or culture can greatly affect the way societies respond to colonizing conditions. For example, the Cherokee, Choctaw, Chickasaw, and Creek all saw the universe as a dualistic struggle between red and white cosmic forces. Social and cosmic harmony and balance were central values in the southeast (Champagne, under review). The Tlingit value of honoring clan ancestors is reflected in their ability to accumulate and distribute wealth in elaborate potlatches. The normative obligation to honor their clan through potlatches motivated many Tlingit to participate in Western market relations; on the other hand, the duality-harmony world view among most traditionally socialized southeasterners inhibited them from engaging in either labor markets or from participating in markets for purposes other than economic subsistence (Champagne, under review; Champagne 1989).

The previous example indicates that the contents of Native American world views vary considerably; there are some general characteristics, however, that may hold for the large majority of indigenous cultures — or at least most Native American societies. The major elements of culture — morality, ceremony, view of causality, and religion — are usually closely interrelated in indigenous societies and in many other societies (Habermas 1981:143–243; Beck and Walters 1977:3–36, 69–91, 277–300). This world view is often revealed in the belief in magic and ceremony; causality is morally and religiously interpreted, and the supernatural world permeates every aspect of culture and society (Hultkrantz 1979:10). The natural order is subject to the powers of the mythical and religious realms, and the laws that hold for humans do not necessarily hold for spirit beings. Native American religions do not emphasize individual salvation or envision sharp tension between this world and the afterworld. Most Native American religions are this-worldly: they emphasize life and reward in the present world. Some exclude the morally destitute (thieves, murderers, adulterers) from a pleasant afterlife and declare that they will be sent to a gloomy existence (excluded as they would be in this world), but their vision is not of a last judgment or divine retribution (Hultkrantz 1979:136).

The general cultural views of nondifferentiated causality, religion, morality, and ceremony, combined with the close connection of the sacred and the profane worlds and the absence of tension between them leads to a traditionalistic orientation toward institutional change (Eisenstadt 1978:101). In many cases, the origins of the world and of societal institutions occurred in the mythical period. Therefore, a society's laws, ceremonies, and institutional order all have mythical ordainments, and well-socialized members will be reluctant to change this order for fear of upsetting the balance. The institutional order and laws of society are considered part of the cosmic order of nature, and are taken as given (cf. Weber 1963:269; Campbell 1976a:5–6, 106, 190–192, 449). In general, because the members of Native American societies have a strong orientation toward preserving culture and institutions, they will probably not initiate change as a way of resolving tensions created in their cultural world views. The primary sources of change will necessarily come from elsewhere.

Nevertheless, as has been shown, traditions will vary considerably in terms of cultural views and a group's inclination toward Western cultural and economic innovations. The materially acquisitive Tlingit were more willing to participate in markets than most southeasterners, who preferred to retain a primarily subsistence livelihood. As will be shown below, some nations will defend institutional configurations that are more differentiated and therefore more accepting of change than others. All else being equal, conservatives in more socially and politically solidary societies will defend an institutional configuration that increases the possibilities of a sustained collective or institutional response to colonial threats; conservatives in societies with only local and particularistic forms of political and social solidarity, on the other hand, will find it harder to form sustained collective or institutional responses to Western contact. The presence of traditionalist cultural orientations does not condemn indigenous societies to a frozen social order; the variation in social and political solidarity, institutional differentiation, geopolitical environment, world-system relations, and Western cultural interpenetration will create variation in the way in which they respond to Western contact.

A Multidimensional Argument

No single-factor argument accounts for the many ways in which indigenous societies respond to Western contact. The variation in institutional change depends on the conditions of the geopolitical environment, the types of markets available, the degree of interpenetration of Western culture and normative order, the continuity of the subsistence economy, the degree and form of social and political solidarity, the configuration of societal differentiation, and the world view and major cultural orientations of the society. A socially and politically well-integrated society which has a differentiated institutional order, which has cultural orientations and values that motivate material acquisition and tolerate hierarchical authority relations, which is subject to a hegemonic geopolitical environment, and which retains a subsistence economic base and has access to markets will most likely adopt a strategy of political and economic institutional change as a way to preserve cultural and national autonomy. On the other hand, a society which has decentralized institutions of social or political solidarity, which has its major institutions nondifferentiated, which has traditionalistic cultural orientations, which has lost its subsistence economic base, which does not have access to new market relations, and which is administratively dominated by a colonizing nation will most likely give little sustained collective resistance and will have great difficulties consensually accepting any major institutional change.

Few American Indian societies fit the institutional change model; many, however, fit the more pessimistic scenario. In practice, numerous combinations of geopolitical, world-system, and sociocultural conditions lie between the two extremes. Today's knowledge of historical social change is such that the outcome of any specific set of conditions is difficult to predict. The previous argument classifies societies according to sociocultural order and colonial context, a classification that at best can only indicate the situational and institutional propensities toward change. More progress can be made if each case and set of conditions is considered in historical context, with an analysis of groups, events, conditions, and institutional relations that make up the historically contingent process of the institutionalization of social change.

The theoretical model indicates where to look in order to understand and analyze how indigenous societies, and societies in general, will change under specific historical conditions. The explanatory power of each of the various arguments can only be determined through analyzing change in empirical societies — a difficult task which requires considerable knowledge of history, social structure, and culture. The arguments presented here can be used to analyze social change in a variety of societies in different historical contexts. More specifically, they can be applied to the study of the institutional change of indigenous societies to colonizing powers in many parts of the world.

Chapter 2

The Iroquois and Delaware in the Northeast

ATIVE AMERICAN SOCIETIES can be divided into several regions based
on geographical, ecological, historical, and cultural characteristics:
the northeast, the southeast, the southwest, the Pacific Northwest, the plains, the Old Northwest, the Great Basin area, Alaska, and
a few others that are less well defined, such as California. Within each
of these regions, we would expect that over the same historical period
the indigenous societies experienced similar geopolitical relations, market
relations, and forms of Western cultural interpenetration; consequently,
these conditions can be controlled. The history and institutional orders
of the societies can help in understanding the ways in which indigenous
societies responded to colonial contact. In the northeast, the Delaware and
the Iroquois are two nations that played important parts in early colonial
history.

The Delaware: Background

At the time of European contact, the Delaware lived in what are now
New York, New Jersey, and part of Delaware. Little evidence exists of
centralized social or political organization among the group. The Delaware
consisted of about 40 different bands that shared common myths, religious
beliefs, and the Lenape ethnic identity, but no national religious ceremonies
or national political commitments or identity. The bands were composed

of several related lineages that camped and hunted together and shared hunting ground rights recognized and respected by the other Delaware bands. The Delaware practiced horticulture: the men helped clear the fields, and the women tended the cultivation and harvesting. Each band had a *sachem*, or leader, who was selected from a group of eligible nephews of the preceding sachem. (Since the bands determined descent through the mother, the nephews inherited the positions of their uncles.) The leader could not exercise coercive political authority, and had to rely instead on his oratory skills, age, proven wisdom, and influence when trying to sway the decisions of the band councils. The sachem was advised by elders from the lineages within the band, while the warriors — men aged 26 to their 40s — stood and listened to the discussions of their elders. The warriors had the right to contribute an opinion, but were held in less regard than the elders of the council. Women did not participate directly in the councils.

The bands might have had an ancient hierarchical order, but these relations are now obscure. When Lewis Henry Morgan visited the Delaware in 1859, he reported that they were divided into three phratries — collections of bands or geographically local kinship groups — and each phratry was further subdivided into 12 kinship groups, for a total of 36 subdivisions (Morgan 1959:51–54; 1977:176–177). Twelve was a sacred number among the Delaware; there were 12 levels to heaven, and one of the central Delaware bands ceremonially sacrificed 12 animals of various kinds in a bonfire (Kenny 1913:193 ff; Kraft 1986:162). Nevertheless, the colonial documents give little direct evidence for the three phratry organizations or the 36 subdivisions. The *Walam Olum*, a set of hieroglyphs that tell the story of the Delaware migration across the North American continent, does not indicate such a division until the very end of the migration, when the Delaware had settled on the East Coast. There the Delaware formed into three divisions — turkey, wolf, and turtle divisions — but there is no mention of the 36 subdivisions. Some scholars question the validity of the Walum Olum; because historical time in the document is obscure, the formation of the three divisions could well have been in the historical period. Little detailed information exists before 1760 on Delaware social structure other than bands and linguistic groupings (Champagne 1988:110).

The available data from the time of European contact indicate that Delaware society consisted of an economically, socially, culturally, and politically decentralized collection of local kinship groups. Because political leadership, band organization, and kinship all overlapped, polity and kinship organization were not differentiated. With the absence of national institutions of social or political cohesion and a nondifferentiated political order, the Delaware do not appear to be candidates for either strong collective action or institutional change in response to Western contact.

Delaware history prior to 1760 indicates that they were indeed hard pressed by the political competition and market relations introduced by European colonies. Throughout this period the Delaware lacked political cohesion, and were militarily defeated by neighboring Indian nations. By 1675 they were subject to the suzerainty of the Iroquois Confederacy. The first regular contacts with Europeans were through the fur trade; by the 1640s, however, the Delaware had overexploited the beaver in their home territory and the Europeans at New Amsterdam preferred to trade with the interior nations. Because the Delaware were not unified or strong enough to force open trade territories from the interior nations, they became increasingly impoverished near the European settlements. They began to sell handicrafts, corn, meat, and land in order to obtain the European goods on which they had grown dependent.

By the 1670s the Delaware bands were selling their home territories and migrating to present-day Pennsylvania near the site where Philadelphia was later built. Between the 1680s and the early 1700s, the Delaware bands depleted the game of the Delaware Valley; some headed west to live near the Ohio River and in the Allegheny region in what is now western Pennsylvania. Colonial and Iroquois pressures for land during the 1720s and 1740s pushed the bands farther west, and the decline of game near the European settlements made them more willing to sell land and migrate. Many Delaware bands lost members to epidemics and joined other bands; their number declined from an estimated 10,000–12,000 at contact to only 2,000 or 3,000 by the mid-1700s (Weslager 1972; 1978). The Delaware bands showed little social or political unity, and appeared to be heading toward further economic marginalization, political subordination, and social and demographic disintegration.

Prior to 1760 no movements had succeeded in institutionalizing major changes in social integration, political unity, societal differentiation, or cultural world view. A major effort for centralizing Delaware political authority was introduced by Pennsylvania colonial officials in an effort to more effectively manage relations with the numerous bands. Between 1718 and 1748 Sassoonan, a leader of a major band, was regarded by colonial officials as "King of the Delaware." Although the officials transacted business through Sassoonan and supported him by giving him authority to distribute material resources, he received only nominal recognition from the Delaware. A dispute over succession in 1747 alienated Sassoonan's nephews from the Pennsylvania alliance, and until the late 1750s the Delaware were reluctant to agree on a leader who would be "fit to undertake to rule a Nation" (Hazard 1851–52:537; Weslager 1972:226–232). Colonial officials' attempts to centralize and rationalize Delaware political order did not lead to any significant change. Before 1760 various Delaware bands had been influenced by Protestant missionaries from the Presbyterian and United Brethren denominations. Probably influenced by these Christian teachings, several prophets emerged during the 1740s and 1750s, but they gained no significant followings and had little influence (Champagne 1988:113–114; Wallace 1956).

The Delaware Revitalization Movement

Throughout most of the colonial period the Delaware bands had been politically and economically allied with the Dutch. After 1664, when the Dutch were defeated by Britain, the Delaware allied with the British colonies. By the late 1750s most Delaware bands were living on the Ohio River or in western Pennsylvania. When the French and Indian War erupted, the western Delaware bands joined the French against the British and participated in raids on the British settlements. By the late 1750s the Delaware and other Indian nations that were allied to the French suffered from lack of sufficient trade goods, weapons, and ammunition. The western Delaware bands were forced to seek trade and alliance with the British. By the end of 1759 the British had gained military supremacy in North America, leading to a new geopolitical situation: for the first time, eastern North America was dominated by a single European colonial power. The possibility of playing the rival colonial powers off one another was no longer available.

The situation of British hegemony created consternation among the Indian nations in the Old Northwest (present-day Ohio, Illinois, Michigan, and Wisconsin). By 1760 most of the Delaware bands had gathered in the Ohio River area, and like the other Indian nations in the region were apprehensive about their future under the British, a situation further exacerbated by British insistence on occupying the old French forts in the interior and by strict regulations on the sale of trade goods, guns, ammunition, and rum to the Indians. The Indians believed that the British planned to annihilate them as punishment for their siding with the French in the late war. Thus, between 1760 and 1763 the Indian nations of the Old Northwest organized and gathered their forces to strike at the British and drive them out of the country (Kenny 1913:187, 192; Heckewelder 1876:290–293).

Several prophets emerged among the Delaware in the early 1760s. One engaged in militant teachings, saying that the Delaware and other Indians had abandoned the ways of their ancestors, sold their land, and adopted European clothes and lifestyles, which had caused the Great Spirit to neglect them and allow them to become destitute. He made the theological argument that the Delaware and other Indians would not reach heaven until they drove the Europeans from their country and returned to the ways of their forebears. This vision was supported by Pontiac, an Ottawa leader who wanted to motivate the Indians to attack the British in the old French forts and drive them out of the country. As a means of mobilizing an Indian confederacy for a military campaign, the prophet's teaching worked quite well. Nevertheless, Pontiac's Rebellion was quickly suppressed, and the militant teachings of the Delaware prophet did not continue to have a significant influence.

The most enduring effects of the revitalization movement occurred in Delaware social organization. By March 1763 the Delaware had formed a national religion that was most likely a synthesis of ceremonies and beliefs previously practiced among the various bands. Only the Delaware were involved in this new religion and members of other Indian nations were explicitly excluded (Kenny 1913:188). The new religion was strongly traditionalistic; it forbade trade with the Europeans and required a return to the economy and lifestyle of their ancestors. It unified three major bands into a common society, religion, and nation. Whether the three phratries were newly created or organized from earlier social forms is not clear. They had coalesced by the late 1750s, but held only an ethnic allegiance; two of the groups did not recognize the third as part of their political organization. The prophet(s) of the new religion integrated the three major bands, created a principal chief, and religiously sanctioned the authority of the phratry chiefs. The prophet created the new chief offices through direct religious revelation: "Our Father has likewise spoke to my chiefs, by me, giving them advice, in what manner to behave as kings, and now they will act as kings" (Croghan 1916:16). Each phratry had a council, a chief, and a head warrior. The turtle phratry was the division of the highest rank; its chief was the principal chief of the nation, and the head warrior of the turtle division served as the nation's military leader.

The major institutional innovations of the Delaware revitalization movement were the religious integration of the society and the formation of institutionalized national political offices. Nevertheless, the society remained nondifferentiated and socially and politically segmentary. The phratry chiefs continued to be selected according to matrilineal kinship rules and the chiefs were leaders of phratries and kin-based subdivisions, which reflected the institutional nondifferentiation of polity and kinship. Furthermore, the three phratries continued to live and hunt in their own territories. The religious integration of the subdivisions superseded and legitimated the new national political organization, which, however, remained politically segmentary and particularistic because each phratry council retained considerable political autonomy. Thus although the Delaware revitalization movement led to the religious integration of the society and the establishment of national political offices, the Delaware polity remained nondifferentiated from culture and kinship. Religious integration did not lead to a political nationality because phratry and local kinship groups continued to command the primary political allegiances of the Delaware. Nevertheless, the Delaware were now more centralized and integrated than they had ever been, and were more capable of unified and consistent diplomatic relations with colonial authorities (Zeisberger 1910:91–112; Weslager 1972:288).

In the next few years after Pontiac's Rebellion, the Delaware phratries continued to have difficulties formulating a national diplomatic front. By the late 1760s, however, the Delaware began formulating diplomatic policies through the national political institutions, a system that remained intact until the American Revolution and the return of competitive geopolitical relations in eastern North America. Early on in the revolutionary war, the Americans sought Delaware alliance or, failing that, Delaware neutrality. The leaders of the turtle phratry favored the Americans, but the wolf leader argued that the colonists presented threats to Delaware land and could not provide trade or military supplies. The turkey leaders were persuaded by the wolf arguments for British alliance. The national council was dissolved; leading members of the turtle phratry fled to the Americans, and most Delaware of the turkey and wolf divisions sided with the British. The wolf leader deposed the turtle leadership for the duration of the war. After the war the national council reprimanded the chief of the wolfs, Captain Pipe, and reinstated the turtle phratry chief as principal chief. This action alienated some of the wolf bands, especially those who had close relations with Captain Pipe.

The end of the revolutionary war did not lead to an end to the fighting on the border. Between 1783 and 1795, intermittent conflicts erupted on the frontier as the Indian nations attempted to protect their territory and block US territorial expansion. In the Old Northwest the British continued to occupy the French forts, which were supposed to have been delivered to the US government through the treaty of 1783. British agents gave weapons and supplies to the Indians in an effort to form the Indian nations into a buffer zone between the United States and Canada. The Delaware helped form a confederation of Indian nations living in the Old Northwest as a way to strengthen their military resistance to the US government and the streams of settlers crossing the Ohio River. During this period of intermittent warfare, the Delaware social structure remained intact, except that the head warrior, usually considered subordinate to the civilian leaders, gained considerable influence over the Delaware warriors.

The fortunes of the Indian confederation—composed of Mingos, Delaware, Potawatomi, Ojibway, Ottawa, Illinois, Shawnee, and others—took a turn for the worse. In the winter of 1794–1795, after the Battle of Fallen Timbers, the British and US governments signed Jay's Treaty, in which the British agreed to surrender the forts of the Old Northwest and end their military support of the western Indian nations. Many Indian leaders were already disillusioned with British alliance because of the unwillingness of British troops to engage in combat at Fallen Timbers. Now the British left their Indian allies to deal with the Americans, and in 1795 the Indian nations were forced to recognize US hegemony over most of the territory east of the Mississippi River.

The Second Delaware Revitalization Movement

In the late 1790s the leaders of the Delaware turtle phratry invited the disaffected wolf bands to rejoin the two other phratries and establish villages along the White River in present-day Indiana, in locations stretching from present-day Indianapolis to Muncie. Even though the Delaware settled farther into the interior, during the early 1800s the American government pressed them and other nations for more land cessions. The pressures created a crisis in Delaware society in 1804, when the three phratry leaders agreed to a land cession that was not approved by the Delaware warriors and people. The turtle chief was deposed, and the chief of the turtle phratry never regained the office of principal chief.

In the spring of 1805, a prophet initiated a revitalization movement emphasizing new ceremonies for the national Delaware religion. The Munsee prophetess, as she was known, was a member of the Munsee nation, which was linguistically related to the Delaware and historically related to the wolf phratry. Her fundamentalist movement emphasized a renewed commitment to traditional institutions and lifestyles, and the rejection of Christianity, of US political institutions, and of the American style of small holder farming (Ferguson 1972:52; Gipson 1938).

Early in the next year the Shawnee prophet emerged, continuing the fundamentalist teachings of the Munsee prophetess and initiating a campaign against witches or anyone who would not accept his teachings. He and his brother, Tecumseh, were residents of the villages along the White River and members of a Shawnee contingent that had been allied to the Delaware since the early 1700s. The Munsee prophetess restricted her teachings to the Delaware and associated groups; when the Shawnee prophet made his debut, she stepped aside in his favor. The Shawnee prophet gained considerable influence among the younger warriors, who were upset over the failure of the Delaware leaders to preserve their territory in the face of US efforts to gain control of the land, and over the declining rate of life expectancy among the Delaware due to deteriorating economic conditions. Thus the movements were instigated by demographic decline, generational tensions, and the failure of traditional leaders to protect the

Indian territories.

The Shawnee prophet initiated a campaign against the civilian chiefs who had participated in the recent cessions of land to the Americans. He planned to replace the old, traditional leaders with warrior leaders and wield them into a unified confederacy to protect the remaining Indian territories from American expansion. Political enemies, elders, and traditional chiefs were accused of witchcraft, and the young warriors moved to execute them under the auspices of the Shawnee prophet, who blamed the accused witches for the causing the present misfortunes of the Indian nations. The Delaware turkey chief had died earlier, but the two remaining chiefs were accused of witchcraft and the deposed turtle chief was executed. According to the teachings of the prophets, the Delaware ejected all resident missionaries and destroyed all agricultural improvements in attempts to return to the economic and social life of their forebears. The movement of 1805–1806 signaled the end of the political structure based on the cultural precedence of the turtle phratry.

Between 1806 and 1810, Anderson, the new chief of the turkey phratry, consolidated leadership over most of the Delaware who did not join the Shawnee prophet. Anderson led the Delaware until his death in 1830, and during his administration the political structure was modified. There was now a principal chief and a second or vice-principal chief, and the three phratries remained the primary political units. The principal chief rule marked some centralization over the earlier political form, and the Delaware retained this political structure for the remainder of their history as an independent nation. Nevertheless, the Delaware political structure remained segmentary, and was not differentiated from kinship organization or from religious symbolic organization.

During the War of 1812, Anderson attempted to keep the Delaware out of the conflict and under the protection of the United States. Many of the Indian nations in the Old Northwest or Great Lakes region joined the British, but the war resulted in their displacement, fragmentation, and decimation. The end of the War of 1812 marked the end of European competition for control of the eastern United States and set the stage for the consolidation of American hegemony over the Indian nations in the interior east of the Mississippi.

After 1817, military resistance was no longer a feasible response to American pressures. Most Delaware attempted to preserve their culture through traditional institutions and lifestyles. The Munsee prophetess religiously legitimated commitments to Delaware kinship and social and economic institutions while attempting to introduce a reformed religious-moral order to offset the corrupting influences of American culture and institutions.

Between 1817 and 1867, the US government periodically pressured the Delaware to move west of the Mississippi. The government, in turn, was pressured by settlers, land speculators, and state and territorial governments. When Congress passed the Removal Act in 1830, the policy became official, and between 1830 and 1845 most of the Indian nations, except some in the original 13 colonies, were displaced to locations west of the Mississippi — many to locations in present-day Kansas and Oklahoma.

Since most Delaware were not willing to accept American farming methods or the teachings of Christianity, they moved west to present-day Missouri and in 1830 to present-day Kansas, retreating to regions where they hoped to continue trapping, hunting, and horticulture. After 1830, the Delaware started hunting buffalo on the Kansas plains. The fur trade remained their primary market.

The Delaware political leadership after 1817 came increasingly under the control of US government officials (Weslager 1972:382–393, 405, 412–421; 1978:221; Ferguson 1972:169), who, through threats and bribes, secured Delaware removal and began to appoint Delaware leaders. Because the officials did not understand Delaware social and political order, they sometimes appointed men to lead a phratry to which they did not belong. Phratry and kinship subdivisions continued to determine political membership, and conflicts between families tended to weaken political solidarity (Ferguson 1972:169). In the 1860s a group of US-supported Christian leaders introduced a constitution and electoral representative government in a failed attempt to differentiate the Delaware polity from kinship and religion and to introduce a more internally differentiated polity. Most Delaware ignored the new government and continued to adhere to their historical forms of political relations (Newcomb 1956:95–104; Weslager 1972:419; Ferguson 1972:166).

After the Civil War, American officials tried to remove the Indian nations from Kansas and resettle them in present-day Oklahoma. They suggested that the Delaware join the Cherokee nation, then located in present-day northeastern Oklahoma. In 1867, after some wavering, the Delaware eventually surrendered their independent political sovereignty and became citizens of the Cherokee nation. Although the Delaware were under pressure from American settlers in Kansas, they were by no means so desperate that they had collapsed as a viable social grouping; rather, their acceptance of Cherokee citizenship was an indication of the influence of the American policies of resettling the Indian nations in Indian Territory, or present-day Oklahoma. After 1867, the main body of Unami Delaware became citizens of and participated in the government of the Cherokee nation. In the 1890s a board was created for the Delaware to pursue claims against the United States for nonfulfillment of past treaties. This body for many years handled business and bureaucratic relations between the Delaware and the US government.

Throughout their history the Delaware showed strong fundamentalist resistance to changing their institutions and culture; the two major revitalization movements in Delaware history created fundamentalist commitments to their institutions. In the post-1760 period, the Delaware showed greater capability to organize against colonial pressures than before 1760, when they maintained a decentralized social, cultural, and political organization. These major innovations brought the religious unification of the three major phratries, but left the Delaware with a polity that was not differentiated from religion or kinship. This nondifferentiated institutional configuration, combined with the explicitly fundamentalist Delaware cultural orientations, proved resistant to the possibility of institutionalizing increased societal or political differentiation or forming a political nationality. Political loyalties remained attached primarily to kinship, regional, and phratry groupings, and political commitments were primarily religious. These fundamentalist orientations resulted in little significant institutional change and only sporadic collective national action in response to US threats to land and national political autonomy.

The Iroquois Confederacy

By 1600, the nations of the Iroquois Confederacy were living in present-day upstate New York, between Albany and Lake Erie. Five nations originally occupied separate territories from east to west: the Mohawk, the Oneida, the Onondaga, the Cayuga, and the Seneca. The confederacy appears to have been founded sometime between 1350 and the early period of Western contact. After 1720, the five nations were joined by a linguistically and culturally kindred Tuscarora nation, which, however, did not receive a place within the confederacy's formal structure (until the nineteenth century) and which relayed opinions through its hosts, the Oneida. The Tuscarora was a nation from the coast in the Carolina colony. In 1712 it became embroiled in a war with the colonists and their Indian allies over trade and debt disputes. Having been ravaged in the war, many Tuscarora decided to migrate north and live with the Oneida.

The institutional order of the confederacy is characterized by the religious integration of segmentary national and kinship groups, and the nondifferentiation of polity, culture, and kinship. The Iroquois Confederacy's structure resembles that of the Delaware after the religious integration of the revitalization movement of 1760, but its organization preceded the Delaware changes. The religious mythology and national and kinship organization of the Iroquois differs from the Delaware, although both groups had nondifferentiated cultural, political, and kinship relations, and religiously integrated segmentary and particularistic political units along with the absence of a political nationality that superseded loyalties to kinship group and region.

According to mythology, the confederacy was created by the demigod Dekanawidah, who was assisted by his speaker, Hiawatha, primarily to alleviate conflict between the Iroquois nations. In Iroquois societies, judicial relations for murder and injury were handled by the various clans. If one member of a clan murdered another member, there was no call for retaliation against the murderer. If someone murdered or accidentally killed someone from another clan within the same nation, then the elders of the clan negotiated a payment for the murder; if no agreement was forthcoming then the murderer had to be surrendered to the victim's clan for execution. The difficulties between the Iroquois nations emerged when a member of a clan in one nation murdered or accidentally killed a member of a clan in a different nation, in which case the clan and nation had to seek revenge on the murderer's nation by killing one of their people. This, however, led to retaliation from the attacked nation and to more deaths.

Dekanawidah had conceived the role of the confederacy as an institutionalized means for negotiating payment for grievances between the Iroquois nations, thereby averting the incessant warfare that was associated under the law of blood. In many respects the ceremonies and goals of the confederacy were primarily socially integrative, an extension of the clan norms of negotiation of grievances to include all the nations wishing to participate. Dekanawidah believed that the confederacy would bring peace to the Iroquois nations. Associated with the Dekanawidah myth was the mission to bring peace to the entire world by incorporating the nations of the world into a peaceful, noncombatant alliance. The symbol of this movement was the Great Tree of Peace, with its white roots of peace spreading to all nations; it was used to draw together an alliance of Indian nations during the 1700s. This symbol is prevalent among conservative Iroquois to this day (Wilson 1959; *Akwesasne Notes* 1978; Erdoes and Ortiz 1984:193–199).

Dekanawidah traveled among the Iroquois nations preaching that the Great Spirit had told him to organize a confederacy and to dictate its constitution and laws as defined by the Great Spirit. The five Iroquois nations joined together and sent several of their clans to the formation. Dekanawidah appointed 49 chiefs, each of whom represented his clan; only those clans present at the formation of the confederacy were assigned chiefs on the confederate council. Not all the nations had an equal number of chiefs, but all the confederate chiefs of a nation combine to make one national vote in the council — so ultimately each nation had a single vote.

The fiftieth chief of the confederate council—the position of Dekanaw-idah himself—did not have a successor. Specific matrilineal, exogamous lineages within the clans of the Iroquois nations determined the succession of the confederate offices. The eldest lineage matron nominated the chief. The chief represented first the interests of his lineage, then of the clan, and, finally, of the nation. The chief was held accountable to the decisions and interests of his kinship group and clan and could be impeached by their consensus. The Iroquois clans were scattered throughout the villages of each nation, and each village had local leaders—often not members of the confederate council—who gained considerable political influence. These leaders were not recognized within the framework of the confederate organization; they did often wield considerable influence over some of the confederate chiefs, however.

Decisions in the confederacy required unanimous consent; they had to be agreed to by the individual lineages, then the clans, then the nation and then by the five nations of the confederacy. If any party dissented on a particular issue, then the decision was not binding. If agreements or compromises could not be found, then each group proceeded according to its own will.

Although the Iroquois through the confederacy had formed institutions of social and ceremonial integration, Iroquois kinship and political institutions were not differentiated, and religious mythology dictated the structure of the Iroquois polity, including the kin-based political organization. Primary political alliances remained tied to lineage and clan and regional groupings. The mythology of the confederacy led to the religious and social integration of segmentary nations and clan and lineage groups, but not to the formation of a political nationality. The direct religious legitimation of the nondifferentiated kin and political organization of the Iroquois Confederacy led well-socialized Iroquois to resist innovations in political, kinship, and cultural order.

Given their nondifferentiated institutional order and primacy of local and particularistic political loyalties, the accomplishments of the Iroquois during the colonial period are remarkable. Between 1600 and 1692 the Iroquois appear to have rarely acted in political unison. The five nations acted independently in diplomatic and trade relations, and one nation was not obligated to come to the defense of another while it was under attack. Between 1649 and 1700, the Iroquois carried on a series of conflicts, known as the Beaver Wars, with the western Indian nations and, at times, with the French. During the first decade of the 1600s, the Mohawk had established trade and diplomatic relations with the Dutch at Fort Orange, and resisted trade relations with the French in New France (present-day Canada). The Iroquois nations soon became dependent on the European trade, and by the 1640s had overexploited the supply of beaver in their home territories. They now looked to arrange trade agreements with the nations deeper in the interior where the beaver populations still thrived. The French, who had trade connections with most of the northern interior nations, moved to influence these nations to reject Iroquois trade overtures because the Iroquois traded with the Dutch. The Iroquois then initiated a series of wars, trying to destroy or coerce into submission the interior nations. Because the Dutch were willing to supply them with guns and ammunition, the Iroquois had an early military advantage, while the French were less willing to supply their trade partners and allies with large quantities of weapons.

After 1666 the British gained control of New Amsterdam, renaming it New York and renaming Fort Orange Albany. The British continued to support the Iroquois efforts to gain access to beaver through diplomatic agreements with the western nations or through force, if required. This military edge enabled the Iroquois to establish a wide range of hegemony over most of the Indian nations in the northeast. Those who resisted were attacked, and several nations were destroyed or forced farther back into the interior of the continent as a result. The Iroquois established the right to hunt in the interior or to act as intermediaries between the British and the western nations. Since the British offered better-quality goods at greater quantities and lower prices, the Iroquois attempted to draw the interior nations away from the French trade.

The Iroquois made some modifications in their organization and strategy during the late 1690s. Prior to 1692, the five nations had always retained the right to speak independently in council through a spokesman (Leder 1956:51–53, 63, 75, 90, 120). But between 1692 and 1701, the Iroquois changed their stance of British-supported trade partner and adopted a new strategy to balance power between the French and British colonies. By the 1690s the Iroquois were on the brink of ruin from the Beaver Wars; between 1696 and 1698, the French launched a military campaign designed to eliminate the Iroquois as a trade and military force in the region. The French and their allies inflicted heavy casualties on the Iroquois, whose position further deteriorated when in 1698 the British withdrew their military aid with the end of King William's War (1689–1697). The Iroquois continued to fight the French, but in 1699 the British claimed sovereignty over Iroquois territory. The Iroquois interpreted this as a direct threat to their national independence and an attempt to exploit their military weakness. Not wanting to live under British rule or become British subjects, between 1700 and 1701 the Iroquois established peace with the French and negotiated an end to the raids by the French-allied Indian nations. They now embarked on a strategy of presenting a unified front to both the British and French, attempting to play a balance-of-power role between the rival

European colonies.

The Iroquois Confederacy now presented a single speaker for all five nations when in council with the Europeans, despite the fact that the five nations had made no fundamental modifications in their decentralized, segmentary, and kin-based social and political structure. The Iroquois also tried to build trade and political alliances with the western Indian nations by binding the western nations into a broad confederacy. In exchange for hunting access, the Iroquois promised the western nations direct access to trade with the British at Albany — an enticing agreement for many. The Iroquois used the Indian confederacy as a means of bolstering their pivotal position between the French and British colonies, by arguing that they could muster all the warriors of numerous Indian nations in the west; in practice, however, the Iroquois had no such influence.

In the 1740s the economic basis of this Indian confederacy began to unravel. Many of the Indian nations in Pennsylvania, including the Delaware and the Shawnee, had migrated west to the Ohio region; the Pennsylvania traders followed them and began to trade deep in the interior. This disrupted the economic means by which the Iroquois had supported the western Indian confederacy. The Iroquois had always restricted British and Dutch trade to Albany, thereby maintaining a monopoly on the interior trade. Now, with the Pennsylvania traders traveling directly to the western nations, the Iroquois' ability to exchange access to trade at Albany for access to western hunting grounds was weakened considerably, and their role as intermediaries — a role many Iroquois had adopted as a substitute for hunting — was undercut. Iroquois political leverage over the confederacy of western nations declined rapidly until the British came to their aid and attempted to gain indirect control over the interior nations through the Iroquois leadership.

Despite the attempt to maintain a united front to the colonists, the Iroquois Confederacy was socially and politically divided. In the French and Indian War (1754–1760), many Seneca favored the French alliance while the Mohawk, long-time British allies, fought with the British. During Pontiac's Rebellion in 1763 some of the Seneca joined the dissident nations, and the Mohawks fought with the British troops who put down the revolt. A critical juncture in Iroquois history came early in the revolutionary war when the Iroquois met to decide whether to ally with the British or with the American colonists or to remain neutral. Significant groups of Iroquois favored all three positions, and the confederate council could not come to agreement; therefore, by the rules of the confederacy, each nation, clan, and lineage decided its own course of action. Some Mohawk immediately joined the British; others remained neutral in their villages. The Oneida and Tuscarora favored American alliance, and the Onondaga favored neutrality. Some Seneca and Cayuga were induced into British alliance by promises of trade goods and ammunition, which the American colonists could not reliably supply. After 1777, because the several nations took opposite sides in the military conflict, the Iroquois could no longer convene the confederate council (Graymont 1972:45–48, 163; Miles 1976:13).

After the war, many of the loyalist Iroquois moved to Canada under the protection of the Canadian government: most Mohawk and Cayuga moved, while many of the Seneca, Onondaga, Tuscarora, and Oneida remained in the United States. The confederate council met occasionally during the period 1783–1812, but there was little political unity. During the War of 1812 the two Iroquois groups fought on opposite sides, and thereafter they formed two separate and independent confederate councils of 49 chiefs. The two confederate organizations for many years thereafter did not meet in council.

During the competitive colonial period, the Iroquois tried to keep a semblance of political unity, but after 1783 and under the pressures of increasing American hegemonic domination, the Iroquois Confederacy fragmented and put up a weak resistance to US demands for territory. Between 1783 and 1797, the Iroquois in New York sold most of their remaining territory to land companies and were relegated to several small reservations of land. Although some of the Iroquois leaders and confederate chiefs resolutely protested the sale of land, the Iroquois population was induced by offers of payment, goods, and promises of perpetual annuities. Neither the confederacy as a whole nor the chiefs of individual nations could prevent the sale of land when overruled by the general population. Attempts to impose restrictions against land sales were ignored or rebuked.

The transition to reservation life brought poverty and social problems, such as alcoholism and the breakup of marital and family relations. The end of the fur trade was in sight, but the men were extremely reluctant to adopt agriculture – for centuries, women had performed horticultural labor. The Iroquois were sullen over their rapid decline from center stage in colonial political relations to political marginalization and domination by the United States. Several leaders advocated different strategies: conservatives argued for maintaining Iroquois culture, and others for acceptance of Christianity and American political and economic institutions. Nonetheless, no concerted mobilization for change was forthcoming.

During the despair of the early reservation period, one of the confederate chiefs, Handsome Lake (or Silver Lake), had several visions. In the first visions, the Great Spirit instructed Handsome Lake to proceed with the moral reordering of Iroquois society; later visions gave instructions for social and economic reforms. Having been in ill health for some time, it was believed that this new prophet had died, gone to heaven, and returned with a message. He quickly gained supporters for his moral reforms against drunkenness and domestic abuse. Between 1799 and 1815 Handsome Lake led a revitalization movement that advocated the social, economic, and religious reform of Iroquois society. He preached that if the Iroquois did not change their ways they would socially disintegrate and cease to remain a people (Wallace 1972; *The Panopolist* 1806–1807:386).

During his ministry Handsome Lake provided religious legitimation for change in Iroquois society. In his view, conformity to the new religious teachings and morality were necessary for personal salvation. The notions of personal salvation and sharp temporal and other-worldly distinctions are not traditional Iroquois views; Handsome Lake borrowed some of his teachings from old Jesuit teachings and more recent missions by the Society of Friends. Handsome Lake renewed commitments to some ceremonies and abandoned others. He gave men religious legitimation to accept the role of farmer, emphasized the nuclear family over clan relations, and induced limited acceptance of Western-style, male-dominated agriculture. On the other hand, he discouraged entrepreneurship and market participation, and advocated that agricultural surpluses be distributed to the old and needy.

In the political sphere, however, Handsome Lake did not make significant changes. Although he gathered early support for leadership of the entire confederacy, no permanent changes occurred in the nondifferentiated Iroquois polity because the other clans refused to give him a central political position, seeing his efforts as an attempt to impose his clan's leadership on the rest of the confederacy. The Iroquois polity, then, remained segmentally organized and nondifferentiated from religious mythology and kinship.

At the end of the War of 1812, it had become clear that the New York Iroquois would have to live indefinitely under American rule. Some Iroquois had argued that the best procedure was to adopt Christianity and American culture, but more conservative members of the reservation communities argued that even if the Iroquois were to accept American lifestyles, they would enter society on the lowest level and never be accorded equal social and civil rights. After 1817 the social and cultural cleavages between Christians and conservatives became increasingly visible, and have lasted to the present day (Wallace 1972:202–208; Carse 1949; Ritzenthaler 1950). Christian and pagan factions divided the Iroquois on most of the New York reservations into two distinct sociocultural communities (Berkhofer 1965; 1977). Both groups struggled for political control and for the right to determine Iroquois social, political, and cultural organization; the culture was, according to our definition, factionally divided.

Handsome Lake's religious teachings were put aside for some 15 years after his death in 1815. They were revived in the early 1830s and used as the basis for a church that continues to have practicing members today. The church was formed by more conservative Iroquois in reaction to what they perceived as the abandonment of Iroquois identity through the adoption of Christianity and American lifestyle among the "progressive" Iroquois. The confederate chiefs organization and the Handsome Lake church became allied in a struggle to prevent the Christians from gaining control of Iroquois society and imposing their cultural and institutional order.

Much of the disunity of the Iroquois nations prior to 1800 was due to conflict within the decentralized order of the confederacy, not struggles over new definitions of political, cultural, or economic order. After 1817 the influence of Protestant Christian missions led to factional cleavages within the Iroquois community. The Protestant missionaries demanded a total transformation of individual moral, social, economic, and political behavior, which entailed the outright rejection of traditional culture and institutions. For the conservative Iroquois, the acceptance of Protestant Christianity meant the loss of Iroquois cultural identity, which was defined by their political and social order and therefore made Christianity unacceptable. Thus the grounds for social consensus and unity between the Christians and conservatives were tenuous (Fenton 1956:577–578; Wallace 1972: 330–336).

During the 1820s and 1830s the remaining Iroquois groups in New York became even more geographically fragmented when they were subject to removal pressures from land companies, New York state, and the federal government. In accordance with the removal policy, the federal government attempted to induce the Iroquois to migrate west of the Mississippi River. By 1817 most of the Mohawk and a large proportion of the American Tuscarora and the Cayuga had migrated to Canada. Most Oneida, and associated Stockbridge and Brothertons, migrated to present-day Wisconsin in the 1820s and 1830s. A small group of Seneca were moved to Oklahoma. Most of the remaining Iroquois fought to remain in their homeland; they succeeded, but at the cost of having to surrender more territory to the Americans. The Seneca reservations were reduced from four to three under conditions that the Seneca considered fraudulent.

The trauma of removal and the loss of the Buffalo Creek reservation led to attempts by the Christians to introduce political reforms and depose the old chiefs, whom they thought were inefficient and incapable of defending Seneca land. Between 1830 and 1848, with the encouragement of the Quakers, the Seneca attempted to introduce a constitutional government. After some abortive attempts at a constitution, which was opposed by the hereditary chiefs, a constitutional government was formed in 1848 for the two Seneca reservations—Cattaraugus and Allegheny. The new government, called the Seneca Republic, was recognized as the official representative of the two Seneca reserves; the third Seneca reservation — Tonawanda — remained under the leadership of the confederate chiefs. During the 1850s and 1860s the confederate chiefs attempted to restore the old political order, but were not strong enough to break the support of the US government for the Seneca Republic (*MH* 1851:14, 100; *MH* 1852:13; *MH* 1859:11, 104, 265; *MH* 1865:154; *MH* 1866:12–13; *MH* 1889: 271; Fenton 1956:568, passim; Fenton 1957:316 ff).

By the late 1880s attempts to form constitutional governments on the Onondaga and Tuscarora reservations failed due to resistance from the majority conservatives. In the early 1890s two-thirds of the New York Iroquois were associated with the conservative or pagan group, the politically predominate group on all the reservations except one (Donaldson 1892:2, 34–44).

In 1892 both New York and Canada passed laws restricting the exercise of traditional governments among the Iroquois reservations and introduced policies of cultural and social assimilation that were strongly resisted by the conservatives. In 1923 the Cayuga chief Deskaheh brought the situation of the Iroquois before the League of Nations in Geneva, but did not succeed in securing support for Iroquois national recognition. In 1924 both Canada and the United States granted the indigenous peoples citizenship, but the conservative Iroquois notified each nation that they would decline citizenship and retain their own nationality and political institutions. That same year the Canadian government abolished the traditional government on the Iroquois reservation at Grand River and imposed an elective government (*Akwesasne Notes* 1978: 89, 92, 108).

All the New York Iroquois rejected the constitutional governments offered by the US government under the Indian Reorganization Act (IRA) of 1934 and the Indian New Deal, in part because they disliked government tactics for inducing them to adopt constitutions, but also because the political forms proposed contained voting procedures, representational government, parliamentary rules and regulations that the Iroquois did not think were appropriate for them (Hauptman 1981:9, 179; *Akwesasne Notes* 1978:89). In 1948 and 1950 Congress granted civil and criminal jurisdiction to the state of New York over its reservations, further restricting the right of self-government within the Iroquois communities.

During the 1950s several Iroquois reservations were targeted for termination under the assimilation policies of that period. The nationwide negative response to termination turned the tide of Indian policy in the late 1950s and early 1960s, and eventually all the reservations escaped dismantling. Nevertheless, the Iroquois lost more land to eminent domain for highways and dams in the '50s. The passage of the Kinzua Dam Act in 1958 resulted in the flooding of much of the land on the Allegheny reservation, and also provided for the termination of the Seneca Republic, although the remaining Seneca reservations have survived. More recently the New York Iroquois have faced the hostility, neglect, and indifference of state, federal, and corporate interests. By the 1970s many Iroquois groups were becoming increasingly sympathetic to activist movements (Hauptman 1986).

Iroquois Traditionalism

The Iroquois communities have survived up until the present day, and the conservatives among them continue to pursue national autonomy and to preserve the cultural and institutional order. The Iroquois response to Western contact has largely been one that has emphasized little change in the fundamental institutional order. The Iroquois Confederacy continues to be the government of the conservatives, and the Handsome Lake church is now a primary center of Iroquois culture. The major institutional changes during the contact period were the economic, social, and cultural reforms introduced through the religious revitalization movement of Handsome Lake. Under duress, the Iroquois required a religiously legitimated modification of their nondifferentiated and segmentary societal order. Otherwise, however, there was little mobilization for the institutionalization of change, despite rapidly changing economic and political conditions. The reforms of Handsome Lake provided a cultural-normative order and economic reform that enabled many Iroquois to manage the transition from an independent horticultural, hunting, and trade society to a dependent, agricultural reservation community.

The Iroquois who accepted Protestant Christianity and American lifestyles advocated a rival institutional order that the conservatives believed threatened Iroquois cultural survival. The Iroquois, with their nondifferentiated institutions and traditionalistic cultural order, were not able to incorporate groups that advocated alternate views; hence, the introduction of American and Protestant religious innovations led to social, political, and cultural fragmentation.

In the end, however, the conservative Iroquois have survived and continue to pursue their national and territorial interests in American courts and within the framework of the international community. The Iroquois strategy for cultural and political survival did not take the path of adopting institutional change to changing political and economic conditions, but rather held strongly to their cultural and institutional order. Only under extreme circumstances, as during the early 1800s, did they adopt, through the Handsome Lake movement, major changes in their cultural, social, and economic institutions.

Northeastern Responses

After the Delaware revitalization movement of the 1760s, the Iroquois and Delaware had relatively similar societal structures: both had religiously integrated, segmentary kinship groups and nondifferentiated political, kinship, and cultural relations. These cultural orientations and institutional configurations resulted in social action aimed at preserving the nondifferentiated cultural-institutional order and responding to Western contact from within the preexisting institutional order.

The major institutional changes came through religious revitalization movements under distressing political and economic conditions and the apparent failure of the old institutional order to cope with the new conditions. Given the decentralized and particularistic political orders of the Delaware and Iroquois, it was difficult to mobilize actions for institutional change even under conditions of economic and political deprivation. Both societies brought about institutional change through religious modifications. Since the religious cultural order played a prominent role in both societies, any changes in political or economic order required changes in religious myths and religious directives. Outside of the religious revitalization movements, there were no other efforts that succeeded in institutionalizing significant changes in Delaware or Iroquois society. These two cases suggest that in religiously integrated, segmentary, nondifferentiated societies, religious revitalization movements are the primary means of instituting change.

The revitalization movements of the Delaware and Iroquois, however, are not typical to the northeastern nations. Most nations in the area had Algonquin cultures: they were organized by decentralized local bands, much like the Delaware before the revitalization movement of 1760. (In fact, many Algonquin groups recognized the Delaware as the "Grandfather" of their nations.) Many of the coastal groups lost large numbers to disease; others, such as the Delaware, grew impoverished as the beaver trade moved west, and many became economically marginalized and lived on the edge of the European settlements. Military resistance, such as was tried in the Pequot War (1637) and in King Philip's War (1675), led to defeat, subjugation, and fragmentation, and many nations near the coast found themselves under European law by the end of the seventeenth century. Nevertheless, no major revitalization movements and little significant institutional change occurred among these coastal groups.

Some groups from the Abenaki Confederacy — Passamaquoddy, Maliseet, Micmac, Penobscot — in present-day Maine and Nova Scotia were allied to the French and accepted French missionaries. Their history seems to be one of relative geographic isolation, continued participation in the fur trade, and, when the fur trade declined, a relatively sparse economic life among the Canadian and American towns in the rural areas of their ancient homeland. They did maintain many of their cultural and ceremonial activities, however. In a court case during the 1970s the Passamaquoddy and Penobscot nations regained the right to buy 300,000 acres of land and received $81,500,000 in compensation for land lost (Brodeur 1985); both nations are now attempting to develop an economic base from the settlement.

Many of the Indian nations of the northeast and Old Northwest experienced forms of economic and political relations similar to those of the Delaware and Iroquois. A common element in the Delaware and Iroquois movements was the influence from Protestant missionaries. Many of the Old Northwest nations and the Algonquin groups in Nova Scotia and Maine had long-term relations with Catholic missionaries. The Catholic Jesuits were often scholarly men aware of cultural and normative variation; they did not seek to impose Catholicism onto the Indians, but rather to reinterpret and synthesize the local culture within the framework of Christian symbols and concepts. On the other hand, the Protestant missionaries considered Indian culture to be heathen, and demanded total economic, cultural, political, and normative transformations from their converts (Herring 1988:103–105).

Although many Iroquois and Delaware naturally found the Protestant teachings unacceptable, they became aware of the Christian concepts of heaven and hell, divine retribution, and personal salvation. The Delaware prior to 1760 had Presbyterian and United Brotherhood missionaries. The emergence of ethical prophets and religiously legitimated mobilization for institutional change were most likely influenced by Protestant missionary teachings, but reinterpreted and incorporated within the Delaware world view. The Iroquois had Jesuit missionaries during the 1660s to 1680s, but only after the arrival of the Quaker missionaries in the late 1790s did they accept the Christian-influenced teachings of the prophet Handsome Lake.

Since both the Delaware and Iroquois had politically decentralized societies and nondifferentiated institutional relations, the possibilities for change were limited. The prophets were successful among the Iroquois and Delaware because they derived their innovations directly from the Great Spirit, which allowed them to religiously respecify some institutional relations within a nondifferentiated institutional order. The prophets also introduced new concepts of moral religious behavior and of personal salvation — which taught that those who refused to comply would be damned — in order to institutionalize their innovations in society. Thus access to and reinterpretation of Protestant conceptions of morality and salvation were critical to the institutionalization of change in both the Delaware and Iroquois revitalization movements.

Chapter 3

The Major Southeastern Nations

T HE NATIONS IN THE SOUTHEAST encountered geopolitical relations similar to those faced by the northeastern nations. The period from 1700 to 1760 was characterized by French, Spanish, and British competition for trade and political hegemony. After a brief period of British domination, competitive geopolitical conditions returned with the American Revolution and lasted until 1795. Thereafter the Americans increasingly consolidated hegemony over the southeast; after 1819 they acquired the Floridas from the Spanish, whereby establishing their claims to the remaining territory east of the Mississippi. The removal policy, formally put into effect in 1830, resulted in the migration of all the major southeastern nations, except for small remnants, to present-day Oklahoma.

Although their geopolitical contexts were similar, the southeast joined the southern plantation export economy after the decline of the fur trade in the early nineteenth century. In the southeast, cotton production and exploitation of slave labor led to the formation of class structures; in contrast, the fur trade prior to 1800 in both the southeast and the northeast did not lead to class stratification. The fur trade, largely controlled by European traders and merchants, did not require new modes or techniques of economic production. Rather, the Indian trappers — and their wives, who did most of the tanning — merely used techniques of production that had been passed on for centuries. In the northeast and Old Northwest, no major alternative commercial markets except for subsistence farming existed after the fur trade declined. Most southeasterners made the transition to subsistence farming and husbandry. A small group, composed primarily of descendants of European traders and of Tories, adopted market orientations and values and were actively engaged in the fur trade. When the demand for cotton expanded after the War of 1812, the entrepreneurial mixed bloods extended their operations into plantation production.

The four major southeastern nations — the Cherokee, Choctaw, Chickasaw, and Creek — made significantly different institutional responses to Western contact from the Iroquois and Delaware. All four southeastern societies formed constitutional governments during the nineteenth century; the Indian nations of the northeast and the Old Northwest made no comparable institutional changes during the same period. The four southeastern nations, however, differed in the rate at which they formed constitutional governments, the use of coercion to achieve this, and the degree of institutional stability.

The Cherokee formed their constitutional government between 1810 and 1827 with little coercion. The other nations did not form constitutional governments until 30-40 years later, under different conditions. The Cherokee formed their constitutional government under intense threats of removal; the other three nations did not. The Choctaw failed in their attempt to follow the Cherokee model in 1830, and the Chickasaw and Creek responded to removal pressures from within their traditional institutional and political orders. The Chickasaw, Creek, and Choctaw formed their constitutional governments only after they were moved to present-day Oklahoma — the Chickasaw in 1856, the Choctaw in 1860, and the Creek in 1867. Although the Choctaw and Chickasaw governments were formed with the aid of coercive measures, both governments became relatively stable. The Creek government proved the most unstable: several rebellions erupted, and the conservatives, who preferred the old government of chiefs, formed a rival government. Because all four major southeastern nations encountered similar geopolitical and world-system relations over the same historical period, the variation in the rate, stability, and use of coercion in forming their constitutional governments was due to differences in cultural and institutional order — differences in the institutional configurations of societal differentiation, and in the forms of political and social solidarity.

The Cherokee

When first encountered, the Cherokee were located in the present-day western Carolinas and eastern Tennessee. The manuscripts from the Hernando de Soto expedition mention a group called Chelaque, but few details are given. According to Cherokee oral history and mythology, precontact Cherokee society was organized as a theocracy and led by priests. A Cherokee creation myth relates that the Great Spirit formed seven clans, generated from his seven sons. Each clan appointed a headman, who was subordinate to the head priest and a council of seven priests who assisted the head priest with ceremonies at the central Cherokee town. The myth mentions village chiefs, village warrior hierarchies, and village councils, but the civil and military authorities were subordinate to the village and national priests. The religious activities of the priests were more important than the activities of the civilian chiefs and councils (*IPH* vol. 9:492; Payne vol. 1:24–28; vol. 3:55–56, 126, 301).

There is a tale of the overthrow of the Cherokee theocracy before the contact period: the oppressiveness of the priests caused a rebellion, which led to their dismissal from positions of leading and central authority (Payne vol. 6:5–6; Corkran 1957:363–364; Longe 1969:10–16). Thereafter, and at the time of British contact in the late 1600s, the Cherokee were organized into a loose confederation of about 60 villages with no central political or ceremonial authority. The national council, composed of village delegations from all the villages, met rarely. Decisions required unanimous consent from all the delegations, and in general there was little coordinated military or political action, since regional and village chiefs often preferred to act independent of other parts of the nation. Primary political loyalties in Cherokee society rested with villages and regions, not to clans or the national council. Consequently, the Cherokee did not have a strong sense of centralized political nationalism.

The seven clans always were central features in the national and village ceremonies, and the duties and activities of performing and preparing for them required the representatives from each of the seven clans (Payne vol. 1:24, 70–75, 80; vol. 4:305, 315, 504). The seven matrilineal clans were represented in all the towns and regions of the nation, and their primary activities regulated private judicial relations among interclan members. The clan heads formed the final judicial body of the nation, but the clans and their headmen restricted their activities and influence to judicial and ceremonial affairs.

The clans were not units of political organization beyond the village (Gilbert 1943:323). In the village, all seven clans gathered to discuss issues of concern, and each clan had a spokesperson who represented its decisions to the village and its leaders. The rest of the village government was composed of a village headman, his assistant, who was also his nephew and from the same clan, the leading members of the warrior organization, and a group of old and influential men recognized for their wisdom and long service to the community. Although clan segments participated in village government, the Cherokee village was a corporate grouping. When the village sent a delegation to the national council, the delegation represented the views of the village community, not those of any particular clan.

Thus the Cherokee clan system encompassed the entire nation and was ceremonially integrated, but its national kinship structure did not have prerogatives in national politics. The Cherokee polity was also relatively differentiated from the cultural and mythical sphere. The Cherokee creation myths ordained the formation of the seven clans and the role and rank of the priests, but left the Cherokee political sphere undefined. Therefore suggested innovations in political organization would not necessarily bring resistance from conservatives wishing to retain the old mythology or culturally ordained political order.

Until the 1760s, Cherokee priests, while having roles that were separate from the village chiefs, were considered influential in major political issues because they were the interpreters of signs from the Great Spirit and his helper spirits from the upper world. The leaders and people respected whatever decision the priests extracted from their divining crystals and other devices; thus the Cherokee cultural orientations influenced political decision making. The Cherokee world view saw religion, causality, ceremony, and morality as tightly bound together. In addition to their belief in magic and in ceremony, the Cherokee believed that to transgress the sacred laws and institutions handed down at creation would lead to worldly retribution in the form of disease, military defeat, death, drought, or some other calamity. Priests played a central role in the ceremonies, such as the Green Corn Ceremony, in which the nation was purified and protected and the transgressions of the past year were washed away (Adair 1775:106–108, 115–116; Longe 1969).

With regard to economic organization, the Cherokee were a hunting and horticultural people. The village community collectively cleared and planted the communal fields each spring, and the women of each lineage household tended the crops of corn, squash, and beans until harvest. At harvest some of the crops were donated to the common village crib, which helped support both the needy and the village government. Each lineage household also kept private gardens. Men hunted and fished, and women gathered wild berries and plants. Most economic activity was designed for local subsistence; little was grown or manufactured for trade.

In terms of economic organization, world view, decentralized political loyalties, and egalitarian political culture, Cherokee society resembled those of many other nations in the southeast. Cherokee institutional order did vary significantly from the other major southeastern nations in terms of national social integration and differentiation of the polity, however. The Cherokee's conception of national social solidarity was ordained through their creation myths, which were reaffirmed through ceremonies. The Cherokee polity, although only tenuously solidary, was differentiated from kinship and from direct mythical specification of the rules and organization of the polity. During the 1700s, Cherokee society became more secularized, the priests were excluded from political influence, and hence the polity separated more from the culture. Cherokee society was perhaps the most differentiated and socially solidary nation in native North America; these institutional features are critical for understanding the relatively adaptive institutional response of the Cherokee to Western impacts.

The first sustained contacts with Europeans came after the establishment of Charles Town in 1670. By the 1690s the British were trading among the Cherokee villages. At first the Cherokee showed little interest in European goods. However, when the British introduced firearms and sponsored a lucrative slave trade in the southeast, the Cherokee quickly found access to guns and ammunition necessary for defense and for slave-raiding expeditions. Indians soon proved to be unreliable slaves; many died from European diseases or used their considerable knowledge of the terrain to flee into the wilderness. The colonists began transporting and selling Indian slaves in the Caribbean Islands, and importing African slaves to work their plantations. By the early 1700s, the slave trade in the southeast began to give way to the fur trade.

Finding the decentralized Cherokee polity of village headmen difficult to work with in diplomatic and trade relations, the British attempted to convince the Cherokee to adopt a single, central authority. Between 1718 and 1752 Carolina officials proclaimed various Cherokee leaders as "emperor" and declined to recognize the authority of any other leaders who would not work through their designated intermediary. The British first recognized a priest from Tugaloo, the sacred Cherokee town where the Great Spirit first gave fire to the Cherokee. After his death a series of warriors were recognized as emperor. From the mid-1730s until 1752, the British recognized Moytoy of Great Tellico and also, later, his son. Great Tellico was a leading "mother town" among the valley towns region. In Cherokee society there were seven mother towns and associated daughter towns. The mother towns had symbolic and limited political authority within their regions. One mother town — Chota, among the overhill towns — challenged the authority and right to national leadership that the British had given to the warriors of the leading valley towns. The "emperor" rank received little recognition within Cherokee political institutions, but carried the influence and support of the British. In the 1820s the leading overhill warriors had been recognized by the British but had lost their influence to the valley town warriors. From the late 1830s on, Chota tried to assume national leadership and British recognition, but was unsuccessful until the early 1750s (Gearing 1962:5, 85–99; Corkran 1970:42–59).

In the early 1750s the leadership of the warriors at Great Tellico was in decline, due to defeat in a war with the Creeks and a trade embargo instigated by Cherokee pillaging of Carolina traders. The head warriors of the valley towns succeeded in reestablishing trade relations with the British, but very little trade flowed into the Cherokee country, and the economic and military crisis deepened. The warrior leaders of the valley towns were discredited, and Chota, now claiming to have been "mother town of the nation," gained broad support for national leadership. The leaders at Chota were not the usual head warriors; instead, leadership was asserted by Old Hop, the crippled and aged headman of Chota. The establishment of leadership at Chota led to the assertion of national political leadership by the village headmen, and the head warriors were relegated to their traditional roles of leaders only in time of war. During the economic and military crisis of 1751 and 1752, the Cherokee villages rallied around Chota, giving it limited authority to negotiate trade and diplomatic relations for the entire nation (Champagne 1983b).

During the 1750s and 1760s, the headmen at Chota attempted to centralize and institutionalize a more regular form of government over the Cherokee villages, an endeavor that ultimately failed. Major difficulties with the British erupted in the late 1750s when, during the French and Indian War, a party of Cherokee skirmished with Virginia frontier settlers and several Cherokee were killed. Upon hearing of the deaths, Chota could not restrain the victims' relatives from seeking revenge on nearby colonial settlements because the clan law was not regulated by the Cherokee government at Chota. The revenge raids led to war with the British in 1760 when colonial militia and British regulars overran many of the Cherokee villages and regions. After suing for peace, the Cherokee leaders sought to strengthen internal political control in order to prevent individual Cherokee from disrupting trade and diplomatic relations with the British.

The British had won the French and Indian War and were now the dominant trade and colonial power in eastern North America. During the 1760s and 1770s, the Cherokee priests were excluded from political and military decision making. They became local doctors and practitioners, and thereafter had little influence in political affairs. The head warrior of the nation usurped the role of head priest, and attempted to use mythical symbolism as a means of centralizing authority and discipline over the Cherokee warriors (Gilbert 1943:366; Dickson 1964:271–275).

Chota's leadership began to unravel at the beginning of the American Revolution. Although most of the village chiefs wished to remain neutral in the conflict, a minority of five villages and a group of young warriors were angered over the loss of land and the continuing colonist encroachments. Consequently, a minority of Cherokee believed that their national interests lay with British alliance and in carrying on the war against the expanding colonial settlements. By 1777 the Cherokee leadership could not restrain the minority from attacking the American settlements, and from 1777 to 1795 the Cherokee country was plagued with intermittent border warfare (Gearing 1962:6, 99–103; Dickson 1964:74, 258–260).

For most of this turbulent period, the dissident warriors and villages — called the Chickamaugas — withdrew from the Cherokee polity and carried on war with the American colonists. Chota's political authority declined and was restricted primarily to the overhill towns, and the individual towns and regions reasserted their political autonomy and carried on independent treaty negotiations and relations with the Americans. During the 1760s and 1770s the village delegations gathered at Chota every autumn for several important ceremonies, but by the 1780s the ceremonies at Chota were less well-attended, and most ceremonies had lost their national character and were instead enacted separately among the villages. The national council met occasionally, but it had little authority.

Then, in 1788, a group of frontiersmen assassinated the principal Cherokee chief, Corn Tassel, and several other leading Cherokee chiefs. This event led to the abandonment of the village of Chota, and motivated many leading warriors and political figures among the overhill Cherokee to join the cause of the Chickamaugas. Thereafter, the Cherokee principal chief was no longer selected from Chota or necessarily from the overhill towns. The selection of the principal chief was now open to candidates from any of the towns and regions, and hence the selection of national leaders became more universal and rationalized. After the late 1780s, the national council often met at Ustanali, a mother town originally located among the lower towns until its inhabitants migrated to the upper towns during the military defeats of the early 1750s.

As the border hostilities continued and the Cherokees suffered casualties, more Cherokee noncombatants entered the conflict primarily to fulfill blood revenge obligations to their fallen kinfolk. An end to the hostilities came in 1795 when both the British and Spanish retired from active politics among the interior Indian nations. The British signed Jay's Treaty, and the Spanish in the Floridas withdrew trade and military support and turned their attention to the Napoleonic Wars in Europe. The Cherokee were forced to sign a treaty with the United States recognizing its hegemony over the region. Between 1795 and 1839, the Cherokee struggled to preserve their traditional homeland and their national political autonomy. Although they had shown some moves toward political centralization during the reign of Chota, these innovations did not survive the borders wars of 1777–1795.

The effort to control the blood revenge failed, too, and Chota declined in political significance. The major institutional changes in Cherokee society before 1795 were the increasing secularization of the polity, where the priests were excluded from the political sphere, and the secularization of the religious-normative order, which affected the political and other institutional spheres (Gearing 1962:103; Dickson 1964:259–260; Gilbert 1943:364–366).

Forming the Cherokee Constitutional Government

After 1795, the United States increasingly pressed the Cherokee to surrender land and to comply with treaty agreements. Two major problems confronted the Cherokee: how to negotiate with the Americans to preserve their homeland and political autonomy, and how to control the blood revenge and thereby prevent a full-scale war with the Americans. In the late 1790s American agents suggested that the Cherokee adopt a law curtailing the blood revenge both against Americans and amongst themselves. Although Cherokee leaders abolished the blood revenge against Americans, not until 1810 did they abolish it among the Cherokee clans.

In the early years of the nineteenth century, the Cherokee were politically divided between upper towns and lower towns, the latter composed of the dissident Chickamauga towns as well as Tories and former traders. The lower towns quickly adopted agriculture and accepted American offers of agricultural implements and advice. The more conservative upper towns at first rejected American offers of economic aid; as the fur trade declined with each passing year, however, they started to adopt subsistence agriculture and husbandry.

The political rift between the two Cherokee regions widened during the period 1804–1806. Some of the lower town chiefs were willing to sell land to the Americans — at times for their own personal gain. The upper town leaders, who wanted to preserve the land, wished to prevent the lower town chiefs from selling land without authorization from the national council. After several unpopular land sales, a prominent lower town chief, Doublehead, was assassinated. Over the next few years, several leaders among the lower towns, believing that it was impossible to stay in the east under pressure for land from the nearby states of Tennessee, Georgia, and the Carolinas, wanted to migrate west. In 1808, several conservative chiefs from the upper towns suggested to the American government that the nation be divided into two separate parts, the lower and upper towns. President Jefferson agreed to this proposal, and the government pressed for division and removal of the lower towns (Henri 1986:256–259; Brown 1938:449–455).

At an 1809 gathering of Cherokee leaders and villages at Willstown during the Green Corn Ceremony, most Cherokee towns declared that they did not want the nation divided into two parts, they did not want to assimilate into American society, and they did not want to exchange their homeland in the east for land in Arkansas. Instead, the Cherokee council announced that the nation had been united, and there would no longer be upper and lower towns. In order to strengthen Cherokee land rights, the council instituted a national committee of 13 members composed primarily of planters, many of whom had some education and could speak English. This committee was assigned the routine business of the national council while it was not in session. From 1809 on, then, the Cherokee formed a political nationality, with the mass of the population committed to preserving their homeland and their political autonomy through a national government and national institutions (Norton 1970:63–76; Wilkins 1986:50).

In the next year, the seven Cherokee clans agreed to forfeit their traditional prerogatives to administer the clan law. Turtle-At-Home, a prominent political figure at the Ustanali council and an instrumental force in the political unification of 1809, signed for the national clan council. The clans agreed to delegate their judicial authority to the national council. With the legitimate use of force now granted solely to the national government, the Cherokee polity became even more centralized. A police force called the lighthorse acted as police, judge, and executioner. The clans continued to exert informal influence over judicial matters and clan norms continued to inform judicial precedents and concepts of justice until well after the Civil War (Dickson 1964:287–290; Wilkins 1986:29–30, 41).

Between 1811 and 1813 several Cherokee experienced visions that expressed doubt about recent economic and cultural changes: the rate of technological change, the abandonment of sacred sites at Chota and Tugaloo, and the cruelty of whipping as punishment for crimes. Several prophets emerged and spread the word throughout the nation, and for a brief period gained considerable support. The prophets forecast that those who did not believe would be destroyed in a fiery hailstorm; they were embarrassed when the prophesy was not fulfilled, and they and their movement were discredited. The Cherokee planters opposed the movement's fundamentalist teachings and argued that if the prophets had their way, all the efforts of the last decade would be lost. Similarly, when the fundamentalist Red Stick Movement erupted among the Creek in 1813–1814, the Cherokee planters actively campaigned to aid the Americans and the Creek lower towns. Although the council was reluctant to join the war, the planters eventually had enough influence to swing the Cherokee into the war against the fundamentalist Creek Red Sticks (McLoughlin 1984).

The end of the War of 1812 marked a critical period in Indian and

American relations. The Americans increasingly dominated the territory east of the Mississippi and south of Canada, and the purchase of Florida in 1819 made the American hegemony complete. Soon after the war, the government actively sought to purchase more land from the Indians. In 1817, 50 Cherokee villages, anticipating another attempt by the Americans to negotiate for more land, met at the village of Amoah to discuss how to strengthen their national government against sale of land by minority coalitions of chiefs. Nancy Ward, the representative of the national women's council, which was composed of a member from each clan, spoke before the council and advocated that the Cherokee continue to make improvements in agriculture and adopt a new form of government. Believing that an all-male constitutional government would better serve the interest of national preservation, the women were willing to sacrifice their traditional right to speak in council. The Cherokee planters also strongly advocated modifying and centralizing the government. The council decided to adopt a short document of written organic law, and enlarged the duties of the national committee to include treaty negotiations and management of land issues with the United States (Foreman 1966:72–79; Tucker 1969:197–198; Payne vol. 6:295–298).

The newly centralized Cherokee government, however, failed to prevent a group of lower town chiefs from signing a removal treaty with the United States in which the Cherokee were expected to either migrate to present-day western Arkansas or take up allotments of 640 acres and become US citizens. Many of the lower town chiefs did not believe that the Cherokee could stay indefinitely in the east under the pressures for land from nearby states, land speculators, settlers, and southern planters. Furthermore, the lower town settlements, which were nearer to the Americans, suffered more from discrimination and economic harassment than did the more isolated upper towns. This act led to the deposing from office of the lower town chiefs, and an effort by the Cherokee majority to rescind the treaty of 1817, since they did not wish to remove or to become US citizens. Most Cherokee viewed the situation as a national crisis, and sent a delegation to Washington City to negotiate a new treaty. After making further land cessions of about 6,000 square miles, the Cherokee gained the Treaty of 1819, which allowed them to retain their remaining territory in the east.

The Cherokee considered the Treaty of 1819 to be a final settlement with the United States. They were resolved to remain on their homeland. About 3,000–4,000 Cherokee had migrated to western Arkansas from 1809 to 1820, but the majority — about 13,000 — remained in the east. During the councils of 1819 and 1820 the Cherokee leaders discussed further changes in the organization of government, and debated the merits of adopting more American innovations.

In 1820 the nation was divided into eight administrative and judicial districts. Villages and regions had always been the primary political units in Cherokee society, but after 1820 the villages no longer played a significant role in Cherokee political organization. The old national council of 50-odd village delegations was now replaced by an elected national council of 32 representatives. The Cherokee also adopted a national court system to take up the burden of hearing cases. The national committee continued to operate as a de facto upper house. This new organization reflected the increased internal differentiation of thé Cherokee polity — the formation of a more independent judiciary, and the differentiation of the Cherokee polity from the social organization of the villages.

Between 1820 and 1827 the Cherokee continued to rationalize their political system. They formed a supreme court, centralized accounting and management of national funds, and passed laws regulating the economy and criminal law. During this period US and Georgia state officials put increased pressure on the Cherokee to sell their remaining land, but the Cherokee held fast. A critical series of events occurred in 1825 and 1826, when William McIntosh, a Creek planter and head warrior of the central Creek village of Coweta, sold much of the remaining Creek land in Georgia to the Americans, but the treaty was considered illegal by the majority of the Creek. Although the Americans did not ratify the agreement, McIntosh was executed under Creek law for illegally selling land. The Creeks were then browbeaten into selling the last of their territory within the chartered limits of Georgia at a treaty in Washington in early 1826. These events whetted the appetite of the Georgia government, which now moved more vigorously to pressure the federal government to remove the Cherokee, the last major Indian nation in Georgia's chartered limits.

In late 1826, the Cherokee national council agreed to hold elections for delegates to a constitutional convention, which was held in July 1827. The Cherokee constitution was ratified by the national council in 1828 and the first elections were held in October of that year. The new constitution was modeled after the US Constitution: it provided separation of powers among the executive, judiciary, and legislative branches, and a legal code that regulated criminal and economic concerns. The Cherokee state was primarily an instrument through which the Cherokee could collectively protect their land, society, and political sovereignty from American encroachments (Perdue 1979:61–62; King 1979:xv; Brown 1938:453). American political pressures led the Cherokee to centralize internal political control and centralize and differentiate their political organization.

This was not an automatic or deterministic response to American political and economic pressures; the Delaware and Iroquois in the northeast, although subject to similar pressures for removal, did not respond in this way. Furthermore, the Creek, Choctaw, and Chickasaw were subject to similar economic relations, formed class structures, and experienced similar political and territorial threats as had the Cherokee. These three groups did not form political nationalities or constitutional governments during the same time period. The national solidarity of the seven ceremonially integrated Cherokee clans and the differentiation of the Cherokee polity from religion, culture, and kinship presented an institutional framework that proved more capable of institutionalizing consensual change than the other, less socially solidary and less differentiated societies.

The Cherokee State, 1828–1907

Between 1828 and 1839 the Cherokee were under increasing pressure to remove west of the Mississippi. The birth of the Cherokee constitutional government had merely redoubled American efforts to drive the Cherokee from their homeland. In 1829 Georgia extended its laws over Cherokee territory, forbidding the Cherokee government to meet except for the purpose of negotiating a treaty of removal or cession of land. The Cherokee remained united, and held their national meetings in lands claimed by Tennessee and Alabama in order to avoid the Georgia militia. The Cherokee were strongly united against removal until 1832, when the decision in the case *Worcester v Georgia* was handed down from the US Supreme Court.

The *Worcester v Georgia* decision was favorable to Cherokee interests, ruling that the state of Georgia could not constitutionally extend its laws over Cherokee territory. The Court did not issue an injunction against Georgia, however, and President Jackson was not willing to enforce the decision, since for the federal government to enforce the Court decision over the Southern states would disrupt relations within an already tenuous political union. The president was not willing to risk civil war in order to uphold Cherokee national and territorial rights (Cochran 1972 [vol. 11]:647–649). He convinced John Ridge, the son of Major Ridge, a planter and pioneer Cherokee leader, that it was not possible to uphold the decision and that the Cherokee should relocate in their own best interests.

Ridge returned to the Cherokee nation in 1832 to pursue a policy of removal west. He was not well received by the majority of conservative Cherokee subsistence farmers, and his plans were rejected by the national party. The Ridges and a group of primarily well-off planters formed the "Treaty Party" to push for removal; the conservative majority, led by principal chief John Ross, opposed removal. In 1835 the Treaty Party signed a removal treaty, but it represented only about 10 percent of the nation and the majority refused to agree. Nevertheless, the US government upheld the treaty, and in 1838 and 1839 forced the majority of Cherokee west, to present-day northeastern Oklahoma. Perhaps as many as 20 percent of the Cherokee population died during the winter march, the Cherokee Trail of Tears.

When the Cherokee arrived in Indian Territory, they were welcomed by the Treaty Party and the Old Settlers, the former lower town Chickamauga group that had previously migrated west. However, they had to submit to the government of the Old Settlers, a representative form of government adopted in 1824. The Cherokee newcomers, led by Chief Ross, argued that they wished to form a convention and create a new, unified constitutional government. After the initial negotiations failed, several leaders of the Treaty Party were assassinated by members of the Ross Party and members of the secret Keetoowah Society (*IPH* vol. 1:36; *IPH* vol. 3:312; *IPH* vol. 14:152–156).

There followed six years of intermittent conflict between the Old Settlers, the Treaty Party, and the Ross Party, or National Party. By 1840 the US government officially recognized the National Party, which contained about three-fourths of the Cherokee nation. The National Party established a new constitution with only minor changes from the 1827 constitution. Composed primarily of conservative subsistence farmers, the party attempted to persuade the dissenting Old Settlers and the Treaty Party to participate in the government. After facing a threat of possible division of the nation by the United States, the Cherokee leaders agreed to a treaty in 1846 that politically united the conflicting groups.

Between 1846 and 1860, Cherokee political relations were peaceful. With the beginning of the Civil War, however, class and cultural cleavages reemerged. With an early appeal for national unity by Chief Ross, the Cherokee initially sided with the South, although many conservatives and members of the newly revived Keetoowah Society opposed slavery and favored a Northern alliance. By 1863, most conservatives had abandoned the Southern Confederacy to fight for the Union; most planters fought for the South.

After the war, the Cherokee were politically reunified through a compromise coalition composed of the Keetoowah Society, led by the Baptist minister Lewis Downing, and selected members of the Southern party (the former planter class). This coalition was called the Downing Party; except for a brief period between 1872 and 1875, when the National Party's William Ross, the nephew of the late John Ross, became principal chief after the death of Downing, the Downing Party candidate won the office of principal chief in the elections from 1867 to 1879. In 1876 the two Baptist missionaries, John and Evan Jones, died. Father and son, both men were key organizers of the Baptist Cherokee within the Keetoowah Society. In the election of 1879, the members of the Keetoowah Society returned to the National Party, and the Downing Party then became the party of the large-scale landholders, ranchers, and merchants. National Party candidates won the principal chieftainship in the elections of 1879 and 1883, but lost a controversial election in 1887, during which American troops had to suppress a possible outbreak of conflict between the two major political parties. From 1887 to 1907, the large-scale farmers, ranchers, American-educated people, and merchants of the Downing Party were elected to the primary offices in the Cherokee government.

Although the Cherokee leadership of the Downing Party did fight to protect national sovereignty, the Curtis Act of 1898 forced the nations in Indian Territory to accept allotment of their common domain and dissolution of their government. Many Cherokee conservatives, reluctant to incorporate into American society, opposed these measures and joined the Nighthawk Keetoowah Society, a conservative wing that claimed that the society was never a political organization but a religious one, instead. The Nighthawks withdrew from political participation within the Cherokee government, which weakened the ability of the conservatives to oppose the more acquiescent Downing Party. The Nighthawks revived ceremonies and clan organization and formed a governmental organization, refusing to acknowledge the right of the US government to abolish Cherokee territory and government. The Cherokee government formally dissolved in 1907, and in 1912 the Cherokee territory was incorporated into the state of Oklahoma.

The Nighthawks still survive today, and the Keetoowah Society continues to operate as a political organization designed to protect the rights of Cherokee nation members (Hendrix 1983:82). After 1907 the US government appointed Cherokee government representatives to manage official business over the remainder of the Cherokee estate. In recent years, the Cherokee have again been allowed the right to elect their own government officials, and have very active elections among their current population, which is about 50,000. At least 10,000 conservative Cherokee still live in eastern Oklahoma, where they are attempting to maintain their communities and culture (Wahrhaftig and Luken-Wahrhaftig 1979). The Cherokee government is now subordinate to the rules and regulations of the Bureau of Indian Affairs.

Cherokee Political Institution Building

Several conditions are important for understanding Cherokee institution building during the nineteenth century: American threats to political sovereignty; a polity that by 1800 was differentiated from culture, kinship, and the institutions of social solidarity; access to the southern export economy; and mythologically and ceremonially integrated institutions of national solidarity composed of the seven Cherokee clans. American threats to territory and political sovereignty made change incumbent on the Cherokee, although the Creek and Chickasaw did not follow this path even though they faced similar political threats during the same period. Incorporation into the southern cotton market led to class stratification among those trader families with entrepreneurial values and orientations. The planters were influential in advocating economic and political change, and introduced American models of political organization and constitutional government. But again, similar class structures emerged among the Creek, Choctaw, and Chickasaw, and none of these societies institutionalized a constitutional government while located in the southeast.

The Cherokee had national institutions of cultural and social integration and, by 1800, a relatively secular polity that was differentiated from kinship and the institutions of mythical-social solidarity. This institutional configuration formed the basis for the relatively adaptive institution building of the Cherokee. Although the mythically and ceremonially integrated seven clans did not provide the basis for a political nationality prior to 1809, the Cherokee formed a politically unified nation when under US threats of removal or assimilation.

The political unification of 1809 was formed with the consent of the seven clans as they gathered for a Green Corn Ceremony, which provided symbolic support and indicated general consensus and agreement. The delegation of judicial procedures to the national government by the seven clans in 1810 brought further legitimacy and consensual support for the political centralization and differentiation of the Cherokee polity. Thus the seven clans provided consensual groundwork for innovations in political solidarity and further political differentiation (Champagne 1983b).

Nevertheless, the Chickasaw had a centralized, mythically and ceremonially integrated kinship structure, but not a polity that was differentiated from culture or kinship. While in the southeast, the Chickasaw did not form a political nationality or constitutional government. They did form one in the post-removal period, but only after their nondifferentiated polity was abolished and they were threatened with national extinction through incorporation into the Choctaw nation. Neither the Creek nor the Choctaw had ceremonially integrated national kinship systems, and neither formed unified political nationalities during removal pressures of the 1820s and 1830s. Consequently, although forming a political nationality required preexisting institutions of national social solidarity, the national ceremonial solidarity within the Chickasaw case indicates that it is easier to adopt political innovations if the polity is differentiated from kinship and cultural institutions.

Thus the Cherokee had two major institutional features that facilitated their capacity to adopt political and economic change: national institutions of social solidarity and a polity that was differentiated from culture, kinship and the institutions of social solidarity. Given the general consensus that was possible among the clans when under conditions of external threat, their externally differentiated polity allowed the Cherokee to consider and adopt innovations in political order without engendering strong opposition from kinship or cultural groups that would otherwise have lost political prerogatives. The major opposition to Cherokee change came from the visionary movement of 1811–1813 and White Path's Rebellion of 1827; both were short lived, however, and did not alter the institutionalization of the Cherokee constitutional government.

The Choctaw

At the time of contact the Choctaw lived in parts of present-day Louisiana and Mississippi. Like the Cherokee, the Choctaw have a myth of the overthrow of a priesthood, which indicates a theocratic societal order perhaps from the mound-building Mississippi Culture that flourished from 900 to 1600 A.D. The Mississippi Culture declined quite rapidly from the time of early Western contact; little is known about it other than through clues gathered from archaeological evidence. According to Cherokee and Choctaw myths and oral history, the priests were overthrown because they had become economically and politically oppressive. The Choctaw elder Chataimataha relates that the Choctaw abandoned living in their central town of Nanih Waiya, most likely a Mississippi Culture town with ramparted defenses and a large mound, because game was scarce (Lincecum 1861:8–9). Sustained contact with Europeans came in the 1680s and 1690s, and the Choctaw were early victims of slave raids sponsored by the British with the aid of Cherokee and Creek raiders. So heavy was the initial onslaught that several major Choctaw divisions suffered near-destruction and large population losses. When the French established Louisiana Colony in 1699, they provided the beleaguered Choctaw with arms and thereafter several Choctaw social divisions held strongly to alliance with the French.

Partly because of the early disruption of Choctaw society, and because early French and British observations leave out many important details, our knowledge of early Choctaw social organization is obscure. It appears that the Choctaw were divided into six major divisions, or *iksa*. *Iksa* was a term that could mean a variety of things: family, local kindred group, chiefdom, or tribe. The six major iksas — Six Towns, Okla Falaya, Immoklusha, Twin Lakes, Chickasawhay, and Kunsha — were divided into two phratries. Kunsha, Twin Lakes, and Okla Falaya consisted of the two symbolically upper division iksas, and Six Towns, Immoklusha, and Chickasawhay formed the lower division. The two phratries managed judicial relations between the major and family iksas. Each major iksa was subdivided into smaller, local, family iksa. The villages in Choctaw society were composed of groups of kindred family iksa. The kinship system was matrilineal and matrilocal, meaning that the man had to travel to his bride's village, and descent and inheritance were reckoned according to the female line. Children belonged to the iksa of their mother (*MH* 1928:214–215; Rowland 1911:237–240; 1907:923–924; *IPH* vol. 51:328).

Kinship, then, was a major organizing principle in Choctaw society. The national and regional councils were composed of village delegations, but these delegations were in turn representatives of local kinship groups – the kindred family iksa that composed the village. Furthermore, the six major iksa were geographically separate, each with its own territory, dialect, and culture. Because one could not marry within one's own village, the six major iksa were bound by intermarriage and culture. Nevertheless, the Choctaw during the period after the 1680s apparently did not gather for national ceremonies; the Green Corn ceremonies were conducted by local villages and clusters of villages that formed chiefdoms.

Economically, the Choctaw were a hunting, fishing, and horticultural people. Most family iksa had fields, which were cleared with the help of the men but tended by the women; men hunted and fished. The division of labor was based primarily on gender and most production was intended for local subsistence.

In Choctaw society social solidarity was local and particularistic. Political commitments went primarily to local kinship and regional groupings. The polity was not differentiated from kinship, and priests did not play a major role in political decision making in the national or village councils (Lincecum 1861:407–409, 475–476).

Internal Choctaw political relations during the first half of the eighteenth century were characterized by shifting alliances among villages and regions that were seeking advantageous trade, military, and diplomatic relations with one of the competing French, British, or Spanish colonies. Chickasawhay, Kunsha, and Six Towns generally favored the French; Twin Lakes tended to favor cheaper, more abundant British trade goods. These shifting alliances bred internal conflict, and in the late 1840s sparked civil war (Rowland 1911:26–28, 245–247; Rowland and Sanders 1927; 1932).

By the early 1750s, the Choctaw iksas had split into three political districts: the southern district, made up of Kunsha, Six Towns, Chickasawhay, and other local iksas; the northeastern district, made up of Twin Lakes and other local iksas, and the northwestern district, Okla Falaya and perhaps Immoklusha. Each of the districts had a head chief, usually a man with many war achievements, and each held a council composed of delegations from the local iksa. A national council, which met rarely, was formed by the gathering of all three chiefs and their councils of "captains" — the headmen of the iksas. All its decisions required unanimous consent, and each district met with the national council only when issues arose that required collective discussion. Consequently, the emergence of three regional political districts did not strengthen national political integration or increase centralization or differentiation of the Choctaw polity (Lincecum 1861:522–525).

After 1795, the Choctaw, like the other southeastern nations, came under increasingly intense pressures for territory and for removal. Significant change in Choctaw institutions did not occur until the 1820s, when the fur trade declined to the point at which it could no longer support most Choctaw hunters. Although American agents had advocated that the Choctaw adopt agriculture and husbandry, most conservatives were reluctant to do so, and as long as the fur trade was viable they had little motivation to change. Beginning in the 1820s, the Choctaw experimented with agricultural, political, and religious innovations.

Like the other southeastern societies, the Choctaw were incorporated into the cotton market; from this emerged a small class of planters and merchants with entrepreneurial backgrounds. During the 1820s, more than 90 percent of the Choctaw became subsistence farmers and husbandmen; they traded limited surpluses, but did not produce primarily for exchange. The market-oriented planters actively promoted education, Christianity, and economic and political change. During this time, the three district governments passed laws that prohibited execution of witches, polygamy, and infanticide, and established schools and a lighthorse police.

A critical juncture came in 1826. William McIntosh, a planter and leading member of the central village of Coweta in the Creek nation, had initiated a sequence of events that led to the sale of all Creek land within the chartered limits of Georgia by February 1826. Fearing a similar sequence of events, the Choctaw councils and young planters, unhappy with the management of government and feeling that the hereditary chiefs would not steadfastly resist US demands for more land, deposed the old chiefs of the northeastern and northwestern districts. In general, the people were dissatisfied with the sitting chiefs because of concessions made during treaty negotiations in Washington in 1825 (Baird 1972:27; MH 1829:187–188; MH 1830:251–253; Edwards 1983:396).

In 1826 the new Choctaw leadership wrote a constitution making the district chiefs elective every four years and creating a national committee for submitting bills to the national council. It introduced laws designed to promote commerce and trade, and tried to abolish some of the Choctaw mores, such as blood revenge, that the Christian missionaries and American agents found objectionable. The Choctaw planters, following a path similar to that taken by the Cherokee, worked to strengthen national resistance to pressures for land and removal by adopting economic and political innovations. In 1828, the chief of the southern district was replaced by a Christian planter, and the three district chiefs proceeded with their plan for national survival (Young 1961:9, 26; MH 1829:153, 382).

In early 1830 the state of Mississippi extended its laws over Choctaw territory and refused to recognize the Choctaw government. Because of state rights and federal government conflicts, President Jackson refused to intervene to protect Choctaw sovereignty according to treaty agreements. In the spring of 1830, the three planter chiefs attempted to strengthen the Choctaw government by establishing a single principal chief; soon after, the leaders bowed to American pressures and signed a treaty of removal. The planter chiefs, observing the economic harassment that accompanied Cherokee resistance, had decided it would be better to negotiate the best possible terms and remove west. The removal treaty, however, was considered too expensive by the US Senate, which rejected it.

In the meantime, the regional leaders led by Moshulatubee, the deposed former chief of the northeastern district, roused a majority opposition to the centralization of the Choctaw government and reestablished district governments. Greenwood Leflore, the principal chief from the northwestern district, attempted to repress the regional chiefs, but failed. Leflore's influence extended only to his district, and the two other districts reestablished district chiefs and deposed the Christian district chief and captains. Consequently, the effort to centralize the Choctaw government failed because regional loyalties and identities were stronger than national loyalties.

In the fall of 1830, the Choctaw leaders were again forced to sign a removal treaty. The new treaty called for removal within three years and included a provision that the Choctaw would adopt a centralized constitutional government soon after establishing themselves in Indian Territory. Since most Choctaw were strongly opposed to removal, by spring of the next year the regional councils of all three districts had deposed their chiefs. The US government, however, refused to recognize any district chiefs or any of the 99 captains except those who had signed the removal treaty. Over the next three years, most Choctaw (about 15,000) removed to Indian Territory, and about 5,000 elected to remain in the east.

Forming the Choctaw Constitutional Government

Between 1834 and 1860, the Choctaw incrementally differentiated and centralized their government. In 1834 the American agent demanded that the Choctaw form a constitutional government according to the Treaty of Dancing Rabbit Creek of 1830. The three political districts had re-formed in Indian Territory, and each of them was politically divided by a majority of conservatives and a minority of Christians and planters. After failing to gain initial cooperation for forming a national government, the agent threatened to seize control of Choctaw national affairs if the Choctaw would not comply with their treaty obligations. The mission-educated Choctaw and the planters favored the proposal; in the summer of 1834, a constitutional government was written and ratified by the chiefs and captains. The new government retained the 33 captains from each district, and, despite American pressure, the Choctaw refused to accept a single, centralized chief executive, instead retaining the three district chiefs who made up the executive branch leadership. Each district retained considerable political autonomy, and the district chiefs did not have authority outside their own districts (M234, roll 170:414–419, 880; Baird 1979:15–16).

A second constitution was adopted in 1838 and allowed the Chickasaw nation to be incorporated as a fourth district, and adopted representational institutions. The number of council members was reduced from 99 to 40, with Apuckshunnubee District having 13 delegates and the other three districts having 9 delegates. This change differentiated the Choctaw polity from kinship, since the 40 delegates were now elected without formal recognition of local iksa groups. Because the districts were dissatisfied with the majority enjoyed by Apuckshunnubee District under the 1838 constitution, another constitution created a bicameral legislature in 1842. In 1850 more changes were made: judicial and administrative districts in the form of 19 counties were introduced, and the judicial administration and supreme court were strengthened. The judicial and legislative branches of the government were now more differentiated, but the executive remained weak and divided among the four politically autonomous district chiefs.

An opportunity for yet another constitutional revision came in 1855 when the Chickasaw withdrew from the Choctaw nation. The Chickasaw had been agitating for separation since the mid-1840s and, although the Choctaw refused to grant separation, the US government intervened and granted the Chickasaw independence through a treaty in 1855. Early in 1856 a convention at Scullyville adopted a new constitution that abolished the old district chiefs and centralized national authority under a single chief executive. The majority of conservative Choctaw protested that the constitution had not been ratified by referendum vote, objected to the abolishment of the district chiefs, and argued that the new political form would lead the US government to form the nation into a territory and incorporate it into the US polity (Baird 1979:18; Debo 1972:74–75).

The Scullyville government gained US government recognition and support, and in 1858 the conservatives formed their own constitution at Doaksville (Debo 1972:75, 155; Berkhofer 1977:142-143). The Doaksville constitution adopted a centralized chief executive, but retained the three district chiefs. American agents attempted to arbitrate, but the conservatives would not abide by procedures for change set out by the Scullyville constitution. The agents then declared the Scullyville constitution to be the recognized government and threatened to bring in American troops.

Having made their commitment to the Scullyville government, the agents suggested that the Choctaw government make concessions to the conservatives by restoring the three district chiefs and allowing a referendum vote on whether to hold a new constitutional convention. The conservatives were satisfied with these concessions, and some of their leaders accepted positions as district chiefs under the government. The referendum vote resulted in a large majority in favor of a new constitutional convention. In the fall of 1859 a leader of the conservative opposition was elected principal chief, and in 1860 a new constitution was adopted with separation of powers and a single, centralized chief executive, but with the three district chiefs retained in limited capacities (M234, roll 175:332-352, 415, 432).

The Choctaw constitution of 1860, modeled after the US government, represented a differentiated polity. It retained the three district chiefs, whose primary function was to keep peace and harmony within their respective districts. The chiefs were to attend the court meetings in their districts and address the people on keeping the law and respecting the constitution. Unlike the Cherokee, who formed a unified political nation before adopting a constitutional government, the Choctaw districts continued to command political loyalties and identities prior to the 1860 constitution. Thus the old district symbols were used to legitimate the new central government. As time passed the principal chief gained more authority and administrative power and the influence of the district chiefs declined, although all attempts before 1907 to abolish the district chief's office failed (Hudson 1939:192-195).

The Choctaw State, 1860–1907

The American Civil War did not divide the Choctaw nation; because of its location and the influence of the Choctaw slaveholders, the Choctaw nation sided with the South. In the post-Civil War period, the Choctaw obtained a stable constitutional polity, in the sense that no major movements or groups challenged the legitimacy of the constitutional form of government. Compared to the Cherokee, political parties among the Choctaw emerged relatively late. Only in the late 1880s, when the US government was pressuring the nations in Indian Territory to allot their land to individuals and dissolve their governments, did two competing political groups emerge. The Eagles, or progressive party, was composed of educated professionals, merchants, market-oriented cattle ranchers and large-scale farmers. The Buzzards, or national party, was primarily composed of conservative subsistence farmers. The Buzzards did not want to allot the common domain or to become incorporated into American society. Although the Eagles, too, were nationalistic, the influx of American settlers and workers spurred by the building of railroads during the early 1870s led many to believe that to resist US intentions of territorialization and statehood for Indian Territory would be impossible. Some outbreaks of political violence occurred in the early 1890s, but this struggle erupted under American pressures to national and political dissolution; it was not a struggle over the institutional form of the Choctaw government, but rather an attack by Buzzards who believed that some of the more acquiescent members of the Eagles had betrayed the nation.

After the Curtis Act of 1898, the Choctaw were forced to accept allotment and the dissolution of their political government. The governments in Indian Territory were abolished in 1907, and the US government took over the management of Choctaw affairs and appointed the principal chief (Knight 1953:76, 85–86; Debo 1972:vii–ix, 129–130, 230). In more recent years, the Choctaw have regained the right to elect a government, but they are now subject to the rules and regulations of the BIA.

Choctaw Political Institution Building

Both the Cherokee and the Choctaw were subject to American hegemonic threats and to missionary and US government efforts for political and economic change, and both were incorporated into the same sequence of world-system relations. Yet the Cherokee formed their constitutional government more than 30 years earlier, and without resorting to force for inducing change. The two societies differed primarily in their institutional order. Although the Choctaw polity was relatively secular, it was not differentiated from kinship organization or from the primarily kin-based institutions of social and political solidarity, making it in general less socially solidary and less differentiated than Cherokee society. The failure of political centralization in 1830 was the direct result of regional groups refusing to acknowledge political centralization, and much of the controversy during the 1856–1858 political conflicts revolved around the issues of political centralization and abolishment of district chiefs. The Choctaw did not form a unified political nationality before they adopted a centralized constitution. In the end, the coercively centralized Choctaw polity required manipulation of regional symbols of social and political integration in order to legitimatize the centralized government.

The centralized Choctaw constitutional government was not formed until after the Choctaw had differentiated polity from kinship during the incremental changes of the 1830s and 1840s. Thus, in 1860, no major obstacles had to be overcome in political differentiation, and the issues of institutionalizing of the centralized government revolved around problems of social and political solidarity. The more differentiated and socially solidary Cherokee, under similar conditions, institutionalized a political nationality and differentiated constitutional government sooner and with less coercion than the members of the less socially solidary and less differentiated Choctaw society.

The Chickasaw

The Chickasaw were found in northern Louisiana and western Tennessee. The de Soto manuscripts mention them as having extensive fields and a chief who was given great deference and carried about in a chair. This view indicates they were part of the theocratic mound-building Mississippi Culture, but accounts in the early 1700s tell of the Chickasaw principal chief being a first among equals with village and clan chiefs, not given any special deference unless he showed great talents in leadership and wisdom. The Mississippi Culture must have been very fragile; it declined quickly after the entrance of the Europeans on the continent (Bourne 1922; Nairne 1988:38–39, 44, 63).

The Chickasaw had a ceremonially integrated national kinship system, and a polity that was not differentiated from culture and kinship. The nation was divided into two phratries which were further subdivided into intermediate iksas and family iksas. Little information exists on the organization of the kinship groups, but some observers say that they were similar to the Choctaw iksas; if such observations are correct, then the Chickasaw iksas would have been local exogamous, matrilineal kinship groups that held rights to local territory, and the villages would have comprised primarily kindred family iksas.

The principal chief, second chief, head and second warrior, national priests, and village chiefs were all hereditary in specific iksas. Thus national political and religious organization were not differentiated from kinship organization. The two phratries and subdivisions were organized into a hierarchy, and when the nation met to celebrate the Green Corn Ceremony, the kin groups camped according to rank order. The national council consisted of the national civil and war leaders, village leaders, and iksa leaders; the council met between the events of the Green Corn Ceremony, and operated like a policy board. All decisions required unanimous consent, and the leaders did not have coercive powers or authority. Priests, who could relay messages between the Great Spirit and the people, were consulted on important political questions. They read and interpreted omens and signs — the communications of the spirit helpers — and delivered them to the people, who generally obeyed them, at least during much of the 1700s (Cotterill 1954:17–21; Steacy 1971:52).

Compared with the Cherokee and Choctaw, the Chickasaw had more centralized national political and religious offices, and the entire nation gathered to celebrate the national religious festivals; the gathering of the national council was secondary to celebrating the national festivals. Neither the Cherokee nor the Choctaw celebrated national religious ceremonies on a regular basis, and most ceremonies were conducted by village or kinship groups.

The Chickasaw played a major part in strategic colonial relations between 1700 and 1760. In 1699 the French implemented a plan to confine the British colonies to the eastern seaboard by building a series of forts and political alliances the length of the Mississippi valley. The Chickasaw were one critical link in the proposed chain of interior alliances, but British traders attempted to keep them as allies. In the late 1820s, the Natchez rebelled against the French; with the aid of the Choctaw, the Natchez were defeated. Some Natchez refugees fled to the Chickasaw for protection, and when the French demanded surrender of the Natchez fugitives, the Chickasaw refused. This incident initiated a 30-year period of constant warfare (1730–1760). The French launched four major military campaigns against the Chickasaw and annually had their Indian allies attack and harass the Chickasaw. Although at times severely beleaguered, the Chickasaw did not surrender their strategic point on the Mississippi, and thereby helped foil the French plan of containing the British colonies (Baird 1974:10–24).

In the years after the Revolutionary War, the Chickasaw were divided in alliance between the Americans and the Spanish. By the early 1790s, American influence began to predominate as the Spanish colonies in the Floridas became weakened by the wars in Europe. During the early decades of the nineteenth century the Chickasaw were pressured to sell their territory in present-day western Kentucky, much to the dissatisfaction of the Chickasaw warriors. The Chickasaw political order remained organized by villages and kinship groups, but the Chickasaw leaders now invited some of the Chickasaw planters and merchants to participate in negotiations with American officials. Members of the Colbert family were most prominent; in exchange for their services, the Chickasaw council allowed them to materially benefit from the treaties. For example, about half the payments for lands ceded in the 1805 treaty went to pay off the private debts of Chickasaw traders and merchants. Some Chickasaw traders inherited national political office, and others received honorary offices for past services. The conservatives within the kin-based national council were willing to allow the traders and planters to privately benefit from the transactions with the Americans as long as the more general interests of preserving territory and national sovereignty were carried out (M234, roll 136:282–283).

Although the planters and merchants became influential in treaty negotiations, they did not propose or attempt to change the Chickasaw polity. Despite the strong removal pressures of the Americans during the 1820s and 1830s, no innovations occurred in political organization. The Chickasaw were overtly fundamentalist, and many rejected Christianity, agriculture, and change in their political system. An American agent among the Chickasaw reported that

> So far from endeavoring to adopt the manner of the whites, if one of them shows a disposition to conform to them, say in dress, he is forced to abandon them or subject himself to frequent insult and his influence amongst them completely destroyed.... [After 50 years of contact with the Americans] they still maintain their old customs, and no argument, however cogent can induce them to depart from them. (M234, roll 135:154–158)

Nevertheless, the decline of the fur trade forced many conservative Chickasaw to adopt subsistence farming and husbandry during the late 1820s. Despite American pressures for territory and removal, incorporation into the southern export economy, and the formation of a merchant and planter class, the Chickasaw did not make any significant change in their kin-based political order. The major changes came in the form of laws designed to promote commerce, protect private property, and uphold contracts (Barden 1953:249; Eaton 1830:7–8; Baird 1974:36).

By the early 1830s the Chickasaw were induced to agree to removal, and by the mid-1830s they were being overrun by settlers and speculators. They could not find a location to which to migrate and settle. As their condition worsened in the east, the Chickasaw agreed in 1837 to pay to be included as citizens in the Choctaw nation and for the right to form a fourth district.

The treaty of 1837 required the Chickasaw to participate in the decentralized Choctaw constitutional government. Many planters and merchants moved to the Chickasaw district, and after some delay formed a district government in the early 1840s. Three rival organizations contended for Chickasaw leadership during the mid-1840s: the conservatives, the planters and merchants, and the Chickasaw Commission. The conservatives, under the leadership of the old principal chief and council, continued to hold meetings. The planters and merchants rejected the old government and adopted the Choctaw constitutional government. The

Chickasaw Commission, formed by the 1834 treaty, had de facto managed most Chickasaw governmental relations since 1834. The primary struggle took place over control of the Chickasaw annuity; the US government ultimately decided in favor of the Choctaw district government. The members of the Chickasaw Commission agreed to resign in 1846, but the conservatives and Chickasaw king, who held a slight majority of supporters, continued to oppose the district government and began to openly agitate for national separation from the Choctaw nation (Baird 1974:50–57; M234, roll 139:141–154, 236–240, 253–254).

According to the American interpretation of the treaty of 1837, the old Chickasaw government was replaced by the elected Chickasaw district government under the Choctaw constitution. The planters and merchants, with the support of American officials, refused to recognize the principal chief or the old kin-based council government. During the late 1840s, the conservatives and planters came to an agreement: the conservatives would agree to accept a constitutional government, and the planters would agree to pursue national separation. In 1846 a short constitution was written, and then a more elaborate constitution was adopted in 1848. In 1850, the Chickasaw elected a "Financial Chief" to manage Chickasaw funds. The chief and government of the Chickasaw district became secondary to the Chickasaw, although still officially recognized by the Choctaw and Americans. Between 1848 and 1855, the Chickasaw, believing that the Choctaw laws were discriminatory and growing weary of boundary disputes and their minority status, sought national independence. The US government intervened and, with a treaty in 1855, the Chickasaw bought the Chickasaw district and were allowed to form an independent government (Gibson 1971:248–250).

The Chickasaw State

In 1856 the Chickasaw formed a differentiated constitutional government with separation of powers between the executive, judicial, and legislative branches. A governor was elected, and from 1856 until the early 1870s the Chickasaw remained nationally unified and planters were predominant within the leadership of the government. During the American Civil War, the Chickasaw remained united, with almost the entire nation siding with the South.

In the early 1870s, the US government asked the Chickasaw government to agree to private division of their common domain, according to clauses from the treaties of 1855 and 1866. The Chickasaw government agreed; according to the 1855 treaty, however, the Choctaw had an interest in the land, and they refused to allow allotment. The Chickasaw leaders' willingness to accept allotment created opposition among the

Chickasaw conservatives, who subsequently formed a new political party: the Pullback, or national, party. The party was made up of conservative subsistence farmers who wished to retain Chickasaw national autonomy and collective ownership of land. The Pullback Party won gubernatorial elections from 1874 to 1896, with the exception of one 2-year term.

By the late 1880s the Chickasaw, with a population of 5,000–6,000, were overrun by American settlers, who numbered well over 150,000 and arrived in greater numbers each year. The Chickasaw conservatives attempted to retain political control, but many Chickasaw were reconciled to the eventual abolishment of the nation. The "progressive" party administrations after 1896 tended to the dismantling of the government and the allotment of the land. After 1907 the US government appointed the Chickasaw governor; since the early 1970s, the Chickasaw have regained the right to elect a government and governor.

Chickasaw Political Change

The Chickasaw were socially well integrated and had national political offices that were not differentiated from kinship and cultural order. They experienced market and geopolitical relations similar to those encountered by the Cherokee and Choctaw. They formed their constitutional government in the postremoval period, about 30 years later than the Cherokee, but before the Choctaw. The Chickasaw did not respond to removal pressures and incorporation into the cotton market with any significant institutional change. They did not form a constitutional government until after the 1840s when the old, nondifferentiated government was abolished by the Americans and by Chickasaw planters, and after the Chickasaw had separated from the Choctaw nation. Thus the Chickasaw government needed more coercion to break down the old, nondifferentiated order than the Cherokee. After the Chickasaw had abandoned the old political order and had formed a unified political nationality, they institutionalized a differentiated national government with less coercion than was required by the less socially and politically solidary Choctaw.

The Creek

In the early 1700s, the Creek lived in present-day central Georgia and Alabama. They did not have a myth of the overthrow of a ruling priesthood; rather, their migration myths tell of the origins of the four central villages. According to one myth, the ancient Creek migration toward the east was a quest to find the house of the sun. After arriving at the Atlantic Coast and realizing the impossibility of their quest, the

Creek decided to remain in the country. The four central villages were the early leaders of the Creek nation. Two villages, Cussetah and Coweta, were the foremost of what the British were to later call the lower towns because they were closer to the British colonies than the Creek towns in Alabama. According to various myths, the principal villages of the upper towns were Abihka, Coosa, Tuckabatchee, and, according to one version, the Chickasaw. The Chickasaw were at one time associated with the Creek during the migration, but later separated off to establish their own nation. The Choctaw have a similar migration myth, which includes both the Creek and the Chickasaw as kindred nations. In the historical period, Abihka and Coosa were closely associated, and by the early 1800s remnants of Coosa had joined with Abihka; the references to Abihka and Coosa, then, probably apply to the same group of leaders or allied villages.

The de Soto expedition encountered Coosa, which then was described as a major chieftainship with a powerful leader and subordinated villages, many of which were recognizable as towns that joined the Creek Confederacy. Coosa, an ancient, central town within the Mississippi Culture, had lost much of its prominence and influence by 1600. The same expedition also describes Talisee as a major chiefdom; Talisee was also a major village in the Creek Confederacy. No mention of Tuckabatchee appears in the de Soto manuscripts, and since its rise to prominence occurred after 1700, the myths that include Tuckabatchee among the original four central towns are probably of late origin. Tuckabatchee was incorporated into the Creek Confederacy when members of the Shawnee nation joined a Creek village (*IPH* vol. 19:432; Grant 1980:326).

The four major Creek towns and all the Creek villages were symbolically divided into red and white towns, a division that reflected the cosmic world view of the Creek and the southeastern nations in general. The upper world—the vault of heaven—was the white sphere, where the Great Spirit and the helpful spirits lived. The lower world, that under the earth, was inhabited by monsters and harmful spirits that crept out of caves, rivers, and springs and caused physical harm to unprotected or sacrilegious humans. Red symbolized fertility, change, strife, danger, growth, and disorder; white symbolized order, age, harmony, cleanliness, purity, and wisdom. The universe was seen as a dualistic struggle between the cosmic red and white forces, and humans, who occupied the middle level, attempted to maintain ritual distinction and balance between the two. The social and political order of Creek society reflected their view of the cosmic order: the red towns ruled during times of war and carried out the duties of police and legislature, and the white towns ruled during times of peace and carried out the duties of executive. In times of peace, the white towns were symbolically superior to the red towns. The four major towns were divided into two red towns and two white towns. In the lower town district, Cussetah was the white town and Coweta was the red town; in the upper towns, Abihka-Coosa was the major white town and Tuckabatchee, after the late 1700s, was the major red town (Swanton 1915:329–330; Hewitt 1939:124–133).

The Creek towns met occasionally at one of the major towns, depending on the business at hand. Decisions were discussed by the village delegations, which, like the Cherokee, represented the views of their village group and not those of their clan or kinship group. All national council decisions required unanimous consent – a frequently difficult task. In disputes over war versus peace, the regions, villages, or segments of villages that favored war gathered their weapons and proceeded to battle, while those that favored peace stayed behind. Although the Creek villages were symbolically ordered, they did not form a unified political or military alliance, but rather formed a symbolically ordered alliance of mutual nonaggression.

Social, cultural, and political loyalties went to the village. Each village with a ceremonial square had a myth of a covenant relation to the Great Spirit, who gave them their laws, ceremonies, and sacred objects. If the people of the village followed these sacred laws and ceremonies, then the Great Spirit protected them from the malevolent spirits of the underworld, thus ensuring peace, victory in war, and prosperity. Breaking the sacred law and rites removed the Great Spirit's protection and benevolence, allowing the spirits of the underworld to bring drought, crop failure, death, disease, and losses in war.

The kinship groups within the village were divided into red and white clans. The red clans were the leaders of the warrior organization, and led during times of war; the members of white clans mastered and led the ceremonies and village civil government. Ideally the leaders of white towns came from white clans, and the leaders of red towns came from red clans, but during the historical period this relation tended the degenerate and the largest clans often assumed control of the village chieftainship. The village kinship groups sat in specified places in the village square where the elders could participate in village business and politics (Hewitt 1939; Swanton 1915:327–328; *IPH* vol. 103:319–322).

Symbolically there were four central Creek clans, and numerous other matrilineal clans and several phratries. Because the Creek Confederacy was composed of numerous villages from different nations and cultures, it had no uniform national kinship system. Extra-village clan and intermarriage ties led to particularistic alliances among the various villages of the nation. None of the Creek clans extended throughout all the villages of the entire nation – as did the seven Cherokee clans – and even the several phratries were local or regional. Furthermore, during the historical period, the Creek did not celebrate a national ceremony.

As did the other southeastern nations, the Creek were engaged in horticulture, fishing, gathering, and hunting. They had a simple division of labor, based primarily on gender: men hunted and helped clear and plant the fields, and women took care of domestic production, tending and harvesting the fields and gathering wild fruits, nuts, and berries. Most production was intended for local consumption by an extended family.

The relation between Creek culture and polity was the least differentiated of the southeastern nations. Creek priests mediated decisions between the people and the supernatural world, and Creek political and social organization was ordered by the dualistic cosmic symbolism of red and white forces. The Creek polity was based on mythically particularistic villages, but the national council was differentiated from kinship as the village delegations represented the interests of their corporate village community and not their kinship group (Hewitt 1939:133). Primary political commitments went to the village community. Consequently, the Creek were socially, culturally, and politically decentralized, with a deep, society-wide interpenetration of cultural symbolism in the organization of the social and political spheres of their society.

Creek Confederacy Building

The Creek villages were encountered by Hernando de Soto, a brief impact that had few long-term effects. The Spanish colonies in Florida had intermittent contact with the Creek, but most Creek villages did not join the Spanish missions, which were destroyed by British and Creek raids in the late 1690s. Some leading Creek villages participated in the slave raids into the Choctaw region, but after 1715 commercial interests turned to the fur trade.

A significant turning point in British-Creek relations came with the Yamassee War in 1715–1717. Trade and debt disputes had erupted between several coastal nations and the British traders, and the British decided to kidnap the family members of hunters who could not pay their debts and use them as slaves. The Creek aided the nations that fought against the British, but the British and their Indian allies, including the Cherokee, defeated the dissident nations, some of which retreated to the Spanish colonies or joined the Creek Confederacy. Chastened by the defeat, the lower town Creek villages migrated from present-day central Georgia and took up residence in western Georgia along the Chattahoochee River.

The Creek then adopted a conscious strategy of balance of power among the local, rival European powers — the French, British and Spanish. Villages from the two major Creek districts often took opposite sides, and the

European colony willing to pay the highest price in trade goods claimed the most Creek allies. At the same time, the Creek leaders avoided any participation in the wars of the Europeans, instead maintaining neutrality.

In addition, the Creek admitted remnant nations from the coastal regions into their confederacy. Many of the Hitchiti villages, and a Yuchi village, a Shawnee village, the Alabama villages, the village of Tuskegee, a group of refugee Natchez and Chickasaw, and others joined the confederacy, often retaining local customs and languages separate from the Muskhogean culture within the Creek Confederacy. Consequently, the Creek Confederacy became a blend of ethnic groups that were symbolically integrated into the Creek political order. Most adopted villages became white towns, with Tuckabatchee, a red town, being a prominent exception. In the case of Tuckabatchee, the Shawnee-speaking immigrants joined an already existing Creek town, which may have been a red town. By incorporating more towns into the confederacy, the Creek leaders hoped to bolster their strategic position among the rival European colonies (Adair 1930:274–278).

Among the lower towns, Coweta formed early trade and diplomatic relations with the British. A few years after the Yamassee War, the British tried to centralize Creek trade and diplomatic relations by appointing one of the headmen of Coweta as emperor of the Creeks. Being a red town, Coweta was not a leader during times of peace, but for the next 40 years this appointment put the town at the center of diplomatic and trade relations. In the upper town region, Abihka and Okfuskie, two major white towns, were the leaders. Abihka, the central actor before the 1750s, became a strong advocate for British alliance while serving as an entrepot for British trade to the Chickasaw and Choctaw. Some upper town villages, like the Alabama towns, tended to favor French alliance, especially after the French built a fort near their villages in 1715. In addition, some white towns among the lower towns sought Spanish alliance in order to offset the British alliance to the red town of Coweta. In general, however, the British enjoyed a trading advantage over the French and Spanish because their trade goods were cheaper, more abundant, and of better quality.

After the end of the French and Indian War (late 1759), the Creek found themselves under political and trade hegemony from the British. Several southeastern nations were calling for an uprising against the British at the same time as Pontiac's Rebellion (1763), but such a revolt never materialized in the south. The Creek and Choctaw became embroiled in a war over hunting territory along the Tombigbee River, and the Cherokee, recently defeated by the English (1760), were not interested in renewing a war against the colonists. Consequently, no militant confederacy could be organized comparable to Pontiac's coalition.

During the period from the end of the French and Indian War to the outbreak of the American Revolution, the British controlled the distribution of trade goods and curtailed any diplomatic gifts while demanding that the Creek earn their trade goods through the market and expected that they assume collective responsibility for disruption of trade relations and for injuries and murder of British colonists and traders. This last demand meant that the Creek leaders had to execute all murderers of Englishmen. In 1763, Coweta resigned its claim to the emperorship, and the British appointed Emisteseguo, a member of Little Talisee, a white town, as the leader among the Creek. Several leaders of upper white towns at Okchai and among the Alabama villages were prominent, but some had favored French alliance, and so the English preferred to work through Emisteseguo, who was influential among the upper towns but not among the lower ones. Coweta became alienated from the British after a member of the tiger clan killed a British trader and Coweta refused to execute him. Emisteseguo had carried out the will of the British in similar cases, but he could not pressure Coweta into carrying out the execution. Eventually, Cussetah executed the murderer, but Cussetah was a white town in which traditionally no blood was to be spilt; it was the duty of the red towns, not the white towns, to carry out executions (Corkran 1967:239–243, 261).

In the 1760s and early 1770s, the white towns were again prominent in Creek leadership. In the lower towns Cussetah and Apalachicola were the central white towns, while in the upper towns Little Talisee and Okchai were the leading white towns, with Tuckabatchee yet to play a central role in diplomatic relations (Corkran 1957:249–258).

The outbreak of the American Revolution led to political divisions among the Creek; most of the upper towns under the leadership of Emisteseguo sided with the British, while several villages led by the white towns of Cussetah, Okfuskie, and Talisee favored neutrality. Other towns were torn internally between neutrality or alliance with the Americans or British. During the early years of the revolution, the neutral party called for the assassination of Emisteseguo and the leading British agents among the upper towns. Being a member of a lowly clan, Emisteseguo had little protection from his kinsmen, and in 1778, in fear of his life, he resigned in favor of William McGillivary, who at the time must have been 18 years old.

McGillivary, son of a Creek mother and a Scottish father who had traded among the leading white villages of the upper town Creek, was educated in Charles Town, and for a time had worked at a trading establishment. Emisteseguo had chosen him as his successor partly because he knew and understood the English language and customs, but also because he was a member of the symbolically central and populous wind clan, providing him with the political allies necessary to protect him from assassination. Strongly favorable to the British cause, McGillivary led the upper town Creek from 1778 until his death in the early 1790s. The neutral and pro-American Creek towns were by 1780 forced to join McGillivary because the American colonies could not supply the goods and weapons that they required. Nevertheless, many of the Creek towns proved unreliable allies, and did not help defend Pensacola and other towns when the Spanish recaptured them in the early 1780s (Corkran 1957:295–323; Cotterill 1954:55–59).

After the revolution the Creek found themselves threatened by American expansion, which McGillivary and the upper towns attempted to staunch by allying with the Spanish in Florida and trading with the British firm Panton, Leslie and Co. Since the Spanish could supply only a few goods, they gave a monopoly to the British firm in order to keep the Indians well supplied. McGillivary also tried to restructure Creek political relations by subordinating the white town leaders to the war town leaders and by placing warriors in the head leadership positions in the town governments. This brought considerable resistance among the old chiefs, who were led by the leaders of the white towns of Cussetah, Okfuskie, and Talisee — the old neutral party. This coalition of dissenting villages made several treaties and land concessions with the Georgia and US governments, but all the treaties were dismissed by the upper towns as unlawful and lacking consent from the national council.

In 1790, McGillivary and 26 towns signed a treaty in New York with President Washington, but McGillivary could not gain agreement among the lower town Creek, who rejected the negotiations. For the last several years of his life, McGillivary tried to create a stronger and more unified sense of national solidarity among the segmentary Creek villages and regions, but he was not successful. He planned to introduce more political innovations, based on the model of the new American republic, but he did not live long enough to carry out his plan. Soon after his death in the early 1790s, the national council restored the old civilian chiefs to national and village authority, and in the end McGillivary's efforts toward political change and centralization were not institutionalized and did not have a long-term impact on Creek political order (Cotterill 1954:56–63).

Early American Hegemony and Creek Removal

After 1795, the Americans were clearly the dominant power in the southeast, and the Creek were forced to acknowledge American hegemony. Among the rivals contending for Creek political leadership, the Americans appointed Mad Dog of Tuckabatchee, rejecting the claims of Hoboithle Micco from Talisee, who had favored the Americans until the late 1780s when he was temporarily incarcerated by the Georgians. Thereafter he became embittered and joined the fundamentalist anti-American Creek villages. Mad Dog led the Creek Confederacy until his retirement in 1803, when he was succeeded by Hopoie Micco of Hickory Ground, an act that in effect returned the leadership to a white town. (According to the American agent Benjamin Hawkins, Hickory Ground was the holiest site in the nation.)

Both Mad Dog and Hopoie Micco favored regular relations with the Americans and also favored the efforts by the US government, through Hawkins, to introduce agriculture, schools, and husbandry into the Creek nation. Hawkins also attempted to change Creek political and normative order: he introduced a police force, attempted to regularize the meetings of the national council, and tried to abolish the blood revenge among the Creek and between Creeks and Americans. The Creek councils of the late 1790s and early 1800s agreed to many of Hawkins' proposals, believing that changes were necessary in order to ensure regular procedures for litigating treaty relations and potential violations (Hawkins 1916:288–299).

In the winter of 1805–1806, Hopoie Micco was assassinated by two men from Cussetah—whether for personal or political reasons the record does not say. The council could not agree on a replacement and from 1808 to 1810, Hoboithle Micco of Talisee vied for leadership. He was recognized by many of the white and the upper towns, but the Americans did not like his fundamentalist, anti-American stance and worked to undermine his leadership by supporting the leaders of the red towns at Tuckabatchee and Coweta. Hawkins was able to remove the Talisee leadership from office by creating a new executive council composed of several upper and lower town chiefs, but led by Coweta and Tuckabatchee (Grant 1980:505–506, 534, 562–565, 579, 587–588).

A major split among the Creek villages occurred with the outbreak of the Red Stick War, which started as a Creek civil war but ended with American involvement. The conflict was instigated by the execution of seven men, mostly members of white upper towns. Led by Little Warrior of Wewocau, these men had killed several American families in Ohio while under the belief that the War of 1812 had already started. The Creek national council refused to join the British or to condone Little Warrior's actions. Hawkins insisted on the execution of the band, which was carried out by warriors primarily from the red towns of Coweta and Tuckabatchee. Although the upper towns had long-standing grievances against land sales and against economic and political change inaugurated by the Americans, and although they were promised military and material support from the alliance of the British and Tecumseh, the dispute over the centralization of a police force and execution of murderers, which violated traditional norms of clan revenge, instigated the Creek upper towns to challenge the American-supported chiefs and call for their deaths (Grant 1980:647; Green 1982:40–43).

The Red Stick War (1813–1814) split the Creek along largely regional affiliations. The upper towns, except Tuckabatchee, Coosa, Abihka, and a few associated towns, sided with the fundamentalist opposition; the lower towns, except the Yuchis, sided with the American-supported council. The war attracted the Americans after the massacre at Fort Mims, and eventually led to the Red Stick defeat despite belated British assistance. The Red Sticks attempted to restore the leaders of the white towns of Talisee and Hickory Ground to Creek leadership; the Americans supported the red towns of Coweta and Tuckabatchee. The defeat of the Red Sticks led to 50 years of Creek leadership by the American-backed central red towns.

After the war, the Americans demanded half the Creek territory — about 10 million acres — and dispossessed many of the Red Stick towns. The national council, led by Coweta and Tuckabatchee, proceeded to abolish the blood revenge and adopted a code of laws. The surviving Red Sticks and returning refugees of the 1820s accepted the new laws, believing that it was not in their power to resist the American-supported red towns.

During the 1820s the Creek government saw more American pressures for land. In 1821 a controversial treaty gave the Americans a large concession, but by late 1824 and early 1825 the Americans were bargaining for the rest of the land within the chartered limits of Georgia. William McIntosh, the head warrior of Coweta, drew up a treaty in February 1825, but it was rejected by the Creek council and McIntosh was executed for treason. The Creek, however, were browbeaten into ceding their remaining land in Georgia early in 1826. The lower town Creek were forced to migrate to Alabama or to present-day eastern Oklahoma. A small group of lower town Creek, who were engaged in the plantation economy and had supported the actions of McIntosh, decided to migrate west between 1829 and 1832. The more conservative white lower towns led by Cussetah remained in the east and reestablished themselves in present-day Alabama.

In 1832, under American federal and Alabama state pressure to remove, and because of large trade debts and drought conditions, the Creek agreed to cede their remaining land in Alabama except for small reservations around their villages where they were guaranteed the right to local self-government. The conservative Creek did not wish to abandon the land of their fathers, and so the treaty of 1832 was a final attempt to preserve the Creek village governments in the east. Between 1834 and 1836 the Creek villages were overrun by American settlers and land speculators to such an extent that most upper town Creek leaders decided to remove west. In 1836 several lower white towns, led by Cussetah and Hitchiti, rebelled against the Alabamans, but were quickly repressed by the US army with the aid of the Creek upper towns. Most Creek were thereafter removed west to present-day Oklahoma (Green 1982:169–186; M234, roll 226: 495–497).

Forming the Creek Constitutional Government

When the Creek arrived in Indian Territory — present-day Oklahoma — they settled into two areas called Canadian and Arkansas districts. The lower towns settled the northeastern segment of the new Creek nation near the Arkansas border, and the upper towns settled in the Canadian district to the southwest. Upon arrival the dissident white lower towns were forced to accept the leadership of Coweta; the upper towns were led by Tuckabatchee. The two districts maintained separate territories, and both had chiefs and second chiefs. At American insistence the two districts met in 1840 and formed a national council that, although it met infrequently, agreed to a code of laws. The two districts remained politically autonomous, and the national council primarily discussed issues that concerned both groups. By the mid-1850s American agents were trying to get the Creek to modify and rationalize their political organization, which continued to be based on village delegations. (Sometimes as many as 800 delegates attended the national council.) In 1859 and 1860 the American agent attempted to institute a constitutional government that would elect a national legislature, abolish villages as primary political units, and separate governmental powers. Although adopted by the Creek council, this constitution was never put into practical effect — most Creek simply ignored it. The proposed constitution of 1860 failed to become institutionalized, although elections were held for several national offices (Swanton 1928:316, 330–332; Debo 1979:124).

The Civil War split the Creek into open conflict, primarily between the upper and lower towns. Most Creek planters and slaveholders lived in the lower towns, which therefore opted for alliance with the South. The upper town Creek, on the other hand, preferred to remain neutral or to ally with the Union in order to preserve their treaty rights. During the war, leaders from white towns assumed leadership, while the leaders of the red towns of Tuckabatchee and Coweta were ignored or relegated to secondary roles. Among the Union or Loyal Creek, the upper town Creek, the longtime leader Opothleyoholo from Tuckabatchee died, and his political influence passed to Sands, a member of Abihka. Among the lower towns, the leadership was assumed by Samuel Checote, a member of a small Hitchiti white town.

After the war, national reconciliation was conducted by the leaders from the white towns. The planters from the lower towns refused to return to the traditional government of chiefs, insisting instead on a constitutional government. The US government supported this and it is said that Sands, believing that the Loyal Creek were the majority, agreed to a constitutional government. (Some conservatives boycotted the convention, but American observers argued that they were the minority.) The speaker of the council at Tuckabatchee refused to obey the new government or honor the reconstruction treaty of 1866 on the grounds that Tuckabatchee was not central to the negotiations. The Loyal Creeks under Sands opted for the new government form. The new constitution of 1867 created a single, principal chief, an assistant, a court system, and an elected bicameral legislature. The villages remained the primary political units in the government and the traditional autonomy of the village governments was preserved (Swanton 1928:330–332; Ohland 1930:48–56).

The new government, however, proved unstable. In 1867, Samuel Checote, who ran with a leader from Talisee, won the first election for principal chief – an election that conservatives claimed was illegal. Sands and the Loyal Creeks withdrew from the new government and formed their own alternative government at the white town of Nuyuka, a daughter town of Okfuskie. The US government recognized the constitutional government, and so the conservatives waited until the next election in 1871, when they descended onto the capital at Ocmulgee and attempted to elect a government through traditional procedures. This action was opposed by the Checote government, which insisted on the validity of election by ballot. The US government intervened and attempted to mediate the dispute. Checote was declared winner of the election, and the conservative opposition was promised a special government commission to investigate its grievances and make recommendations to settle Creek political differences. The commission, after hearing the position of the various Creek parties, ultimately decided that the conservatives should honor the new constitutional government. The Loyal Creek then sent delegates to the national government, except for Wewocau, a white town (Ohland 1930:56–58).

In the election of 1875, the conservative candidate Lochar Harjo was elected principal chief over Checote by a wide margin. He served only briefly: the legislature impeached him for violating the constitution. Although Harjo's impeachment was engineered by the large-scale landholders and cattle ranchers, even some of the conservative legislators voted for his impeachment. Gathering his supporters at Nuyuka, Harjo again claimed they would not obey the constitutional government and threatened to have himself reinstated as principal chief. The remainder of his term in office was served by the second chief, Ward Coachman, who formed the Muskogee Party with a coalition of freedmen and conservatives who were willing to accept the constitutional government. In the election of 1879, Checote ran against Coachman; according to oral tradition, the conservatives at Nuyuka ran Isparhechar for principal chief. Checote won by a small margin, but the conservatives led by Isparhechar disputed the election.

The disgruntled conservatives again formed their own alternative government and challenged the American-supported constitutional government. Between 1881 and 1883, sporadic incidents erupted into the Green Peach War, which ended in defeat for the conservatives. The conservatives were forced out of the Creek nation into the Sac and Fox country, where American troops subdued them and after several months persuaded them to return to the Creek nation. Isparhechar and his men were obligated to swear an oath to the constitutional government, and from Nuyuka they planned to campaign for the election of 1883 (*IPH* vol. 2:231). The results were again disputed. Isparhechar's men controlled the legislature, but in early 1884 the US government declared the Muskogee Party candidate, J. M. Perryman, the winner. Legus Perryman of the Union Party won the elections of 1887 and 1891, but was impeached for malfeasance before the end of his second term. The impeachment scandal disrupted the Union Party, and in the election of 1895 Isparhechar was elected principal chief. Isparhechar's term saw the introduction of the Dawes Commission into Indian Territory, which advocated the private sectioning of the Creek national domain and the abolishment of the independent Creek government. Although Isparhechar opposed US efforts to abolish Creek government, he was unable to prevent it. The Creek administrations after 1899 oversaw the implementation of the American acts to allot land and dismantle the Creek government. From the mid-1890s into the first decade of the twentieth century, a conservative group centered at Hickory Ground opposed allotment and the extinguishment of the Creek government. The group ultimately was forced to accept allotments, and on several occasions its leaders were arrested when American troops and marshals were called in to maintain order. The members of the fundamentalist movement were called Snakes and were led by Chitto Harjo.

After 1907 the US president appointed the Creek principal chief, who managed the remainder of the business attached to the Creek estate. In the mid-1930s the Creek accepted and organized under the IRA Act. Many of the Creek villages had survived as social, ceremonial, and political units. The new IRA government was organized along lines that preserved the autonomy of the villages, although thereafter the Creek government was subject to the rules and regulations of the BIA.

The Creek institutional configuration—decentralized relations of social and political solidarity organized through red and white cosmic symbolism and particularistic religious covenant relations—proved the most resistant to change among the major southeastern nations. The Creek were the last to adopt a constitutional government, and were the most unstable in the sense that major groups formed alternate governments and moved to dismantle the constitutional government and reinstitute the old government by chiefs. The Creek had more disturbances over the organization of the government and faced more use of coercion to maintain order than any of the other southeastern nations.

Social Change in the Southeast

The four major southeastern nations can be compared under conditions that approximate a natural experiment. All four nations were subject to similar world-system relations starting first with the fur trade, then the southern plantation-export system, and finally the export economy of the Indian Territory. Furthermore, entrepreneurial classes emerged in all four nations during the early 1800s. All four nations were subject to similar pressures for land and removal from the United States during the nineteenth century. Thus, the variation in rate and form of institutional change cannot be accounted for by world-system, class, or geopolitical arguments. The latter arguments are preconditions to the institutional changes that take place among the southeastern nations, but they cannot by themselves account for the rate of and variation in the formation of differentiated constitutional governments.

In each society, the market-oriented planters were foremost in pressing for economic, political, social, and cultural change. However, the planters were not strong enough to force change on the majority of conservative subsistence farmers, although the US government was instrumental in dismantling the old governments among the Chickasaw, Creek, and Choctaw and in maintaining internal order among the Creek and Choctaw. The Cherokee, given the pressing economic and political conditions, largely accepted change in economic and political order; among the Chickasaw, Creek, and Choctaw, however, American agents in alliance with Indian planters resorted to coercion in order to create more centralized and differentiated polities.

The Cherokee had a ceremonially integrated national kinship system, and by 1800 their polity was differentiated from religion and kinship. Under American pressures for cession of land the Cherokee formed a political nationality, and between 1809 and 1827 formed a centralized and differentiated constitutional government. The Chickasaw, too, had a ceremonially integrated national kinship system, but their polity was not differentiated from kinship and culture. The Chickasaw mounted considerable resistance to institutional change during removal pressures, and formed a political nationality during the 1840s after the planter-American alliance discarded the old form of government. Nationalist orientations led to a separatist movement; with the help of the US government, an independent constitutional government was formed consensually in 1856. The Choctaw society was decentralized socially and politically, and the polity was not differentiated from kinship. The Choctaw planters had difficulties centralizing the polity over the resistance of the conservatives. The Choctaw formed their constitutional government at an incremental pace, led by planters and American agents. Forming a centralized constitutional government required coercion and the manipulation of traditional regional symbols. The Creek, with their decentralized social and political institutions and symbolically ordered social and political organization, were the most resistant to institutional change; conservatives, who preferred the old form of government, had to be forced to participate in the constitutional government.

The northeast had no large-scale slave and plantation market, and none of its societies became class stratified during the nineteenth century. In addition, no national constitutional governments were formed in that region. The Seneca Republic represented only two Seneca reservations, not the entire Iroquois Confederacy. Even Seneca conservatives argued that the Seneca Republic would not have survived were it not for American recognition and support. The Delaware and Iroquois were culturally integrated societies whose political orders were mythically specified, making them most comparable to the Creek and early Chickasaw societies, although kinship organization and world view varied considerably among them. Like the Creek and early Chickasaw, the Iroquois and Delaware showed considerable resistance to institutional change. After the breakdown of the nondifferentiated Chickasaw polity, the Chickasaw showed willingness to change their political order as a means to ensure national independence and survival. During the nineteenth century, the more secular Choctaw and Cherokee were the most active in introducing institutional change, but the less differentiated and solidary Choctaw were unable to consensually institutionalize a centralized constitutional government until more than 30 years after the more socially and politically solidary and differentiated Cherokee society.

Chapter 4

The Plains

N OW WE MOVE TO the ecological zone of the societies of the Great Plains. Although many contemporary American perceptions of Native Americans derive from the imagery of the plains nations, most of these societies moved to the plains only relatively recently.

Many of the plains nations from the 1800s, such as the Osage, Pawnee, Sioux, and Cheyenne, were horticultural or woodland Indians before they adopted the plains nomadic lifestyle of following and hunting buffalo. The Great Plains societies had a different economic base than that of the horticultural and hunting societies of the east. By the early 1800s, the plains nations had become specialized in the hunting of buffalo and other game, and their traditional emphasis on horticulture had almost disappeared. The specialization into buffalo hunting, which also was accompanied by religious, cultural, and social reorientations, is a major factor in understanding the rapid changes brought on by American contact.

In the eastern horticultural and hunting societies, the period of sustained contact with the West was prolonged over a period of more than two centuries. This contact did not result in the destruction of the horticultural economic base, but it was accompanied by the decline in game for subsistence and trade. The destruction of the vast buffalo herds and the rapid American expansion following the Civil War did not provide the plains nations with time or resources with which they could make sustained institutional or collective responses. By the 1890s most plains nations were relegated to small reservations with no viable subsistence base, and were being pressured by the US government to enact economic, political, and cultural changes.

The archetypal vision of the decline of the plains nations is one of a precipitous decline in morale and degrading economic and bureaucratic dependence on officials of the Office of Indian Affairs. For a time it was thought that the Indian nations would quickly die out and that those who survived would be assimilated into American society. The disappearance of the plains nations, however, did not come to pass, although the plains nations in the reservation period are often characterized as institutionally fragmented and politically factional.

The Sioux, for example, are often characterized by their residence on several separate reservations; even within the same reservation there are disputes over the proper form of government – traditional, based on tiyospaye leaders, versus democratic, based on the IRA governments. The more conservative Sioux remain loyal to their hereditary band leaders, and the more American-educated and entrepreneurial Sioux, who have accepted at least some American values and lifestyles, are willing to work within the context of the reservation political framework that has been set down through the BIA (Schusky 1975:193, 225; Powers 1977:222; DeMallie 1978:276). The Sioux have experienced internal disputes over different rules of political organization; without an underlying consensus, the Sioux reservation tribal governments appear unstable and dependent on American support.

This factionalism is not inherent to the plains area, but rather depends on the social orders of the nations in the plains region. In the case of the Sioux society, which had a ceremonially integrated society during the brief annual Sun Dance but otherwise was organized into decentralized and segmentary kin-based groups, there were marked differences in the forms of social and political solidarity and differentiation of the polity that are prerequisites to institutionalizing the secular national solidarity and nonkin–based polities that the BIA has imposed upon the Sioux and other plains nations. Without normative and institutional congruence and community consensus over the form of political order, many Sioux reservation governments remain only partially institutionalized.

Sioux society represents only one institutional configuration among the plains societies; others have social and cultural institutions that vary considerably from the Sioux political order. Those societies with more solidary and differentiated institutional orders should exhibit more institutional and collective adaptations to reservation conditions. The Crow, Northern Cheyenne, and Northern Shoshone will provide contrasting examples to the political fragmentation that is observed in many of the Sioux reservation communities.

The Northern Cheyenne

In the early European contact period, the Cheyenne, an Algonquin-speaking people, were probably located in mid-eastern Canada. Forced by European expansion and intertribal warfare to migrate to present-day Minnesota and then subsequently out onto the plains during the latter half of the 1700s, their society was composed of ten traditional bands. With their transition to the plains culture based on buffalo hunting came a religious movement that reorganized Cheyenne ceremonial, political, and religious life.

Sometime around the year 1775, a prophet named Sweet Medicine gave the Cheyenne a sacred bundle of four arrows and established a code of sacred laws deemed to have been handed down directly from the Cheyenne supreme being, Ma?heo?o, or the Creator. Sweet Medicine brought a covenant from the Creator to the Cheyenne people; if the Cheyenne would adhere to the laws and ceremonies transmitted by Sweet Medicine, then the Creator would ensure the cultural and national survival of the Cheyenne nation. The sacred arrow bundle symbolized the covenant relation with the Creator; as long as the Cheyenne kept the arrows in good condition and ceremonially renewed them each year, they would prosper. Two arrows symbolized control over animals to ensure good hunting, and the other two symbolized control over man.

The sacred arrows, which pervade all aspects of Northern Cheyenne society, are symbolic of unity and communication with the Creator (Powell 1969:580). In the Cheyenne world view, the sacred arrow bundle was the greatest resource for ensuring cultural and national survival (Whiteman 1973:1). The prophet Erect Horns, from the Suhtaio band, brought the Cheyenne the Sacred Buffalo Hat and the Sun Dance. The Sun Dance ensured world renewal, and the ceremonial care of the Sacred Buffalo Hat ensured tribal survival and well-being.

Because the Cheyenne were a peripheral people who were forced to flee across half a continent to avoid the onslaught of the European colonial expansion (Hoebel 1978:1-13), their concerns for physical and cultural survival were reflected in their cultural and religious orientations. The Creator had a purpose for every Cheyenne, but enlightenment to the Creator's purpose and meaning could only be gained through the ceremonial and sacred life of the tribe (Woodenlegs 1979:50). Northern Cheyenne cultural orientations were this-worldly, emphasizing tribal well-being and day-to-day survival; Northern Cheyenne society had no individual, other-worldly salvation, as in Christianity, but it did have a belief in transformation or transmigration. Those who acted against the Cheyenne moral-religious order, or who died in a bad way — that is, a death irrelevant to tribal ends—forfeited their right to reincarnation or spiritual participation in the tribal community (Straus 1978:1). Consequently, the individuals who contributed to tribal preservation ensured that future generations of Cheyenne, and their own transmigrated or spiritual existence, would have a place in the tribal community. The spirits of the Cheyenne were believed to advise and participate in tribal society even after death. This emphasis on cultural and physical survival was institutionalized in religious and ceremonial activities and internalized by each person through belief in reincarnation and spiritual participation in tribal life after death (Straus 1978:3-4).

In traditional Cheyenne society, the religious sphere legitimated and defined the political order. When the prophet Sweet Medicine handed down the Creator's laws, he included some for the organization of a Council of 44 Chiefs. Every decade, each of the 10 bands would select four leaders, usually the headmen of the largest lineages within the bands. Four men from the group of retiring chiefs were selected by the new council to serve as "Old Man Chiefs," and one man from the new group of chiefs was selected to be the Sweet Medicine Chief. A primary purpose of the Council of 44 Chiefs was to organize the annual religious ceremonies and buffalo hunt, the only two events during which the plains Cheyenne gathered communally; during most of the year, they were divided into the 10 bands at different camping and hunting locations. The council made political decisions, but only after consulting with the four warrior societies, which implemented the council's decisions.

The organization of the council was believed to have been directly given to the Cheyenne by the Creator himself. When in council, the circle of chiefs were believed to be directly communicating with the Creator through his intermediary, the Sweet Medicine Chief. The negotiated and unanimous decisions of the council were directly and explicitly legitimated by the Creator (Whiteman 1973:2; Powell 1980:54-60; Hoebel 1978:18, 48-49). The council was headed by a religious figure and many if not most of its decisions were on ceremonial matters.

The Cheyenne had a religiously integrated political structure; kinship ties were not formally recognized as an organizing principle of the Council of 44 Chiefs. The 10 traditional bands were composed of lineage groups, but membership in a band was made by choice, not by kinship affiliation. The largest lineages usually led the bands and selected their own kinsmen for chieftainship in the Council of 44 Chiefs. While kinship did not have a formal place within the religious laws that formed the council, it was important politically within the bands. When a man addressed the council, it was assumed that he spoke only in behalf of his extended kinship group.

The Council of 44 Chiefs did not manage the tribal economy. At the annual buffalo hunt, the council designated one of the soldier societies to police and organize the hunt. Throughout the year, bands and kinship groups managed the gathering of their own economic subsistence, and Cheyenne values and norms regulated the redistribution of wealth from the more successful hunters and war leaders to the orphans, the elderly, and the poor.

Bureaucratic Domination

Prior to 1850, the Cheyenne had split into two groups — now called Northern and Southern Cheyenne — as one group migrated to the south in order better to exploit buffalo-hide trading opportunities. The Southern Cheyenne took the sacred arrow bundle; the Northern Cheyenne retained the Sacred Buffalo Hat. After an unsuccessful attempt to resettle the Northern Cheyenne in present-day Oklahoma, in the early 1880s the Northern Cheyenne were allowed to settle on a reservation in eastern Montana.

Between 1880 and 1934, the Office of Indian Affairs implemented a policy of assimilation. The traditional Northern Cheyenne chief and warrior societies were ignored in favor of US bureaucratic officials, who managed local governmental functions and tried to turn the Northern Cheyenne into farmers and husbandmen, and of missionaries, who tried to educate and christianize them. Cheyenne ceremonial and religious life, now suppressed, was forced underground (Powell 1969:339–341). Although the chief and warrior societies were excluded from political authority, they retained traditional forms of political influence on the reservation and helped organize the preservation of the Cheyenne sacred bundles (Powell 1969:394, 1981:1,276). In 1937, the Northern Cheyenne voted to accept a constitutional government under the provisions of the Indian Reorganization Act of 1934 (IRA), although many traditional Northern Cheyenne opposed it as an American attempt to destroy the old, sacred form of Cheyenne government (Powell 1981:1,276). The political influence of the traditional chief and warrior societies steadily declined, and both societies became more concerned with ceremonial functions and were largely excluded from secular political decision making.

The Northern Cheyenne IRA tribal government is subject to BIA regulation. The BIA and the Secretary of the Interior have the right to review all tribal council decisions and to veto or modify them if they do not conform to policy. In effect, the BIA, as a result of its assimilation mission, controls schools, training programs, and economic infrastructure, and regulates tribal government economic decision making. Because of treaty obligations, the BIA is responsible for ensuring that Northern Cheyenne land and natural resources are used in the best interests of the tribe, and

BIA officials are obliged to guard against any transaction that would result in the permanent loss of land or unfairly encumber the economic resources of the Northern Cheyenne. The Northern Cheyenne, therefore, depend on the BIA to monitor and approve their contracts. Through this control, the BIA often makes the major productive resources available for exploitation to American corporations (Boggs 1984; Cornell 1984:44).

Northern Cheyenne Society Today

Many of the cultural, religious, and nondifferentiated aspects of early Cheyenne society survive today. Northern Cheyenne culture, values, and kinship affiliations remain relatively intact and independent of economic marginalization and dependency and of a formally secular and differentiated IRA tribal government organization (Nordstrom et al. 1977:25, 134, 208–210; Weist 1977:211). The teachings of the prophets, the sacred bundles, and the ceremonies are still an integral part of contemporary life for most Northern Cheyenne (Whiteman 1973:3), and the theme of cultural and physical survival through preserving tradition and through participating in ceremonies continues to inform contemporary Northern Cheyenne social action (Owens and Boggs 1977:13; Nordstrom et al. 1977:3, 112–143; Erdoes and Ortiz 1984:204–205).

Northern Cheyenne tradition does not sanction self-interested accumulation of wealth; the "giveaway" remains the primary means of redistributing wealth. Instead of giving away horses, as was done in the past, nowadays food and kitchen and household items are given away. At powwows and funerals, families pool their resources and give away "tables" loaded with gifts. The ideal giveaway is one to the poor, from whom no reciprocal gifts can be expected (Weist 1973:101). The community continues to value sharing and egalitarianism (Owens and Boggs 1977:21; Owens and Peres 1980:78; fieldwork).

The Cheyenne emphasize cooperation, sharing, generosity, religious spirituality, and tribal welfare, all of which conflict with Western notions of economic rationality and American materialistic values (Owens and Boggs 1977:27). "Efficiency and profit orientation characterize outside development interests; . . . Cheyennes think first about the present and past welfare of their people, Tribe, culture, natural resources, and homeland" (Nordstrom et al. 1977:146). Obligations to kin and social relations are more important than making money or attending work regularly (Nordstrom et al. 1977:182; interviews). To save or to accumulate wealth is not congruent with Northern Cheyenne kinship obligations to aid relatives and friends in need (Owens and Peres 1980:48; interviews), and most Northern Cheyenne continue to evince a precapitalist labor ethic (interviews; Owens and Peres 1980:21–22).

Tribal Government and Economy

The IRA government is formally secular. Although the Cheyenne religion and ceremonies do not directly inform the political action of the IRA government in the same way that they informed the decision making of the traditional Council of 44 Chiefs, the contemporary IRA government does maintain links to the Northern Cheyenne religious and ceremonial sphere. For example, the IRA tribal government sends representatives to the annual sacred arrows ceremony held by the Southern Cheyenne of Oklahoma. It gives a salary to the keeper of the Sacred Buffalo Hat, which is located on the Northern Cheyenne reservation, and the chief and warrior societies also receive small grants. The tribal government also contributes to giveaways, and to organizing and financing the annual Sun Dance (Liberty 1965:131 ff).

More acculturated Northern Cheyenne view the tribal government as a secular organization, but the traditional members of the tribe still believe that Northern Cheyenne religion, praying, and ceremonies should give guidance, purpose, and meaning to the tribal government (interviews). John Woodenlegs, tribal chairman for more than 20 years and president of the local chapter of the Native American Church, firmly believed that Northern Cheyenne religion was the means to political and social integration (interview, NCTR). Since his death, recent tribal chairmen have not used traditional forms of spiritual guidance to inform their political actions, and some of the conservatives believe that the Northern Cheyenne have lost direction and political unity. The conservatives hope that the importance of religion in the tribal government will be reestablished (interviews; Powell 1981:1,273–1,275).

Kinship and neighborhood or old band alliances continue to command the social allegiances of Northern Cheyenne tribal members (Nordstrom et al. 1977:110, 121); the basic social unit in Northern Cheyenne society is still the extended family (Weist 1977:201). The bureaucratic rules and regulations that the BIA enforces on the tribal government often contradict these traditional normative injunctions (Owens and Peres 1980:49). In the economically depressed Northern Cheyenne economy, individual and family ties sometimes supersede tribal ties, and this creates internal competition and factionalism (Liberty 1965:129). For example, tribal council members often chose their own relatives for tribal government jobs and program benefits (Tribal Council meeting 4/18/83).

In addition to the religious, kinship, and locality influences on the tribal government, the tribal government must also include the Northern Cheyenne community in any major decisions. The IRA government formally delegates political authority to the tribal council, but the Northern Cheyenne community is reluctant to delegate decision-making power to a small group of men. "(T)hey do not think it is desirable to have a small group of men make their decisions . . . they feel very strongly that all segments of the Cheyenne population must be involved in the decision-making process" (interview, NCTR). The IRA constitution allows a referendum vote on all tribal ordinances and resolutions; if the community is dissatisfied with a decision, it can petition the tribal council, which then must hold a referendum vote. Consequently, major economic decisions such as whether to allow strip mining or drilling for oil on the reservation are decided by community discussion and vote. Routine political decision making is delegated to the tribal government, but major decisions that will affect the community are decided by negotiation and consensus.

From the standpoint of external differentiation of the polity, Northern Cheyenne religion, kinship, locality, community norms, consensus, and interaction inform political decision making. The Northern Cheyenne IRA tribal government also evinces an internally nondifferentiated governmental organization. The relations between the judicial, executive, and legislative branches overlap, and they are dominated by the tribal council or legislative branch. Most of the decision making within the tribal government resides with the elected tribal council, and the tribal chairman generally makes proposals and chairs the council meetings. The bureaucratic administration of the tribal government is conducted by an executive committee and subcommittees of the tribal council. The powers between the tribal council and the tribal administration are diffusely defined. Attempts to create rules and regulations that would define relations of authority between the legislative and administrative branches must be first passed by the tribal council and have been voted down in recent years (1980–1983) (Tribal Council meeting 2/28/83). Furthermore, the IRA constitution gives the tribal council plenary power over judicial affairs. The tribal courts do not have power other than that which the tribal council explicitly delegates to them (Tribal Council meetings 2/28/83, 4/18/83). Consequently, lawmaking, law enforcement, and legal interpretation tend to originate in and are subject to the decisions of the tribal council. The council members, however, are embedded in a web of kinship and political and local community demands that are consequently not insulated from tribal bureaucratic and judicial administration (Tribal Council meeting 2/28/83; PCIRE 1984:29).

Economic Development

According to Pringle (1958:67, 77), the efforts prior to 1950 to create a self-sufficient economy on the Tongue River reservation, through subsistence farming, cattle raising, and support from New Deal programs, ended in failure. The Northern Cheyenne became largely proletarianized, unemployed, and dependent on government aid. Although the small endowment of arable and grazing land helps account for the limited success of these efforts, Pringle (1958:77, 88–93) argues that Northern Cheyenne cultural conservatism and institutions also inhibited their willingness to accept economic change. Although they were as willing to work as anyone, the Northern Cheyenne, with their religiously informed, consensual, and egalitarian forms of leadership, had difficulty managing hierarchically organized economic or bureaucratic organizations (Pringle 1958:77–78).

Pringle argues that despite Northern Cheyenne poverty, even existing reservation resources were not used effectively. He attributes the unwillingness to maximize exploitation of reservation economic resources to the influence of Northern Cheyenne culture and values. By the 1950s, the old chief and warrior societies were still influential over most Cheyenne, Cheyenne religion was very much alive, and Cheyenne values and norms regarding material gain still were contrary to Western norms of economic rationality and accumulation of wealth (Pringle 1958:86–88, 92).

During the 1960s, the tribal government's major economic strategy was to buy back all reservation lands that had been sold to non-Cheyennes. By the early 1980s, 61 percent of reservation land was controlled by the tribal council, 37 percent was controlled by individuals who had inherited land from the reservation allotment in the 1920s, and about 2 percent was fee simple (NCTR). The tribal council regained grazing rights to 88 percent of the reservation surface, which can support from 12,000 to 13,000 head of cattle. Prior to the 1960s, much of the Tongue River reservation grazing land was leased to non-Cheyennes by the BIA. The long-term strategy of regaining tribal government control over all the reservation land is congruent not necessarily with the tribal government's desire to bring it under economic production but rather with its concern for controlling the land base.

The two major economic events in recent Northern Cheyenne history have been the controversy over coal development in the 1970s and the ARCO deal for drilling oil in the early 1980s. Both of these events illustrate how the Northern Cheyenne made decisions based on ecological, economic, political, community, and cultural considerations.

By 1973, the BIA had signed coal mining leases with six energy companies, leases that encompassed 56 percent of the Tongue River reservation surface. The leases contained relatively low royalty rates (17.5¢ per ton), and proposed electrical generating plants on the reservation (Boggs 1984:211). The reservation contained an estimated 5 billion tons of strip-minable coal deposit, and American energy policy was aimed at exploiting these reserves and thereby reducing dependency on foreign energy sources. In 1973, the tribal council was approached by an energy company that wanted to make coal leases directly with the tribe rather than passing through the BIA intermediary. The BIA normally made and monitored all Northern Cheyenne coal leasing arrangements. The energy company proposed to strip-mine coal and build coal gasification facilities, a project that would at least temporarily attract about 30,000 non-Cheyenne construction workers onto the reservation. The reservation population was no more than 3,500.

The tribal council, quickly realizing the threat looming over the Northern Cheyenne community, submitted a legal petition in 1974 to the Secretary of the Interior for cancellation of the coal leases on the Tongue River reservation. The petition cited more than 30 violations of Department of the Interior rules and regulations concerning leasing contracts, and the Secretary was compelled to suspend the leases. Among the gross violations were failure to undertake environmental impact statements and leasing of many of the tracts in excess of the 2,500-acre limit. The secretary ruled that the lease contracts would have to be renegotiated between the Northern Cheyenne tribe and the energy companies. The Northern Cheyenne have refused to renegotiate any commercial coal leasing contracts with any of the companies, effectively nullifying the earlier BIA-negotiated leasing contracts.

The Northern Cheyenne, an impoverished group, stood to make millions from the coal leasing agreements (Hoebel 1978:132; Boggs 1984:221–222). Community opposition has been so strong, however, that the tribal council cannot consider renegotiating the contracts. A sample survey showed that 80 percent (N=342) of the Northern Cheyenne did not want to see the land disturbed by coal mining (Nordstrom et al. 1977:171). During the 1970s the Northern Cheyenne tribal council went into debt by employing attorneys to oppose nearby off-reservation coal mining and electrical generating plants that could adversely affect the reservation ecology (Boggs 1984:223). Some members of the newly elected council in 1978 favored coal development and in the summer of 1979 two coal companies approached the Northern Cheyenne with a partnership offer to develop strip mining. The companies offered $3 million on signing the contract, and more than $1 billion in Northern Cheyenne profits for the next 20 years. The plan failed to get widespread community support, however, and no contract was signed (*Akwesasne Notes* 1980:19). Instead, the same tribal government leaders turned their attention to oil development and signed an agreement with ARCO. Conservative opposition groups eventually forced the tribal government to put the question to a referendum vote, as stated in the tribal constitution, and in the summer of 1980 the referendum vote favored the oil drilling contract, which promised an up-front per capita distribution of

$1,500. Consequently, the Northern Cheyenne rejected coal development by widespread community consensus, but a majority were willing to accept oil exploration on the Tongue River reservation (Boggs 1984).

As already noted, an estimated 80 percent of the Northern Cheyenne opposed commercial coal development. A survey revealed that 66.8 percent of the Northern Cheyenne thought that commercial coal development would improve reservation economic conditions. They expected more and better-paying jobs, more local businesses, improved financial conditions for the tribe as a whole, and an improved standard of living. Thus it is clear that the Northern Cheyenne had an appreciation for the economic and material benefits that would derive from coal development.

One of the greatest Northern Cheyenne fears was that the influx of outsiders associated with coal development would greatly reduce their chances of passing their culture on to succeeding generations or even surviving as a people (interviews, NCTR; *Akwesasne Notes* 1980:18; Nordstrom et al. 1977:164-165). Coal strip mining threatened to destroy the land that had been won through great sacrifice by their ancestors. Land is symbolic of Northern Cheyenne physical and cultural survival (interviews, NCTR; Nordstrom et al. 1977:174-175), and some conservatives believe that the land, because of its symbolic and sacred role in Cheyenne religion and history, should not be used for commercial purposes (Boggs 1984:235). The Northern Cheyenne elders warned that outsiders would eventually control and own the reservation and politically subordinate the Northern Cheyenne people (interviews, NCTR). The conservative Northern Cheyenne were willing to forego immediate and substantial economic gain if it meant that economic development would threaten their homeland, institutions, political autonomy, and culture (Chestnut 1978:167; Bird 1983). The more entrepreneurial cattle ranchers on the reservation joined the conservatives in opposing strip mining because the ecological effects threatened to harm the ranchers' livelihood.

The acceptance of the agreement to allow ARCO to drill for oil on the reservation, then, cannot be merely attributed to the offer of $1,500 per capita by the oil company. The conservatives who opposed the oil contract were unwilling to pursue any resource development, but they were overwhelmingly defeated in the 1980 referendum, indicating that the conservatives, although a vocal and significant force on the reservation, were in the minority. Most Northern Cheyenne were willing to accept oil extraction because the economic benefits were clear and it did not threaten the land base, reservation political autonomy, and Northern Cheyenne culture (Boggs 1984:228).

During my field work on the Northern Cheyenne reservation in the winter of 1982-1983, most of the tribal council members who had negotiated the

ARCO contract had been removed from office and the majority of the council was ambivalent toward the agreement, often citing examples of how the oil drilling upset the reservation water tables and ecology. Because the price of oil has plummeted in recent years, the external pressures on the Northern Cheyenne to sell their natural energy resources have abated. There is little interest currently in Northern Cheyenne coal; ARCO has a long-term contract to drill Northern Cheyenne oil, although preliminary drilling did not show positive results.

The Crow

The Crow are now located on a reservation in eastern Montana that starts on the western boundary of the Northern Cheyenne reservation; both groups were subject to similar opportunities for coal and development during the 1970s and early 1980s. Like the Northern Cheyenne, the Crow wished to preserve their sacred sites and ecology, but the Crow have a much more active orientation toward economic development than do the Northern Cheyenne. The Crow community at large is more willing to allow coal mining and oil extraction and to consider coal gasification developments on its reservation. This difference in perspective derives largely from differences in culture, political order, and institutional relations.

During the 1800s the Crow were a plains group that hunted buffalo. Although they were linguistically related to the Sioux, the groups were bitter enemies. During the buffalo hunting days, Crow social organization was composed of bands and 13 matrilineal clans. According to myth, each clan had a name given by the Creator in his manifestation as the trickster-creator figure, Old Man Coyote (Frey 1987:40–41, 178). The clans have dwindled to eight, but they remain a central feature of Crow social organization. The clans were informally paired with a tendency for marriages between matched pairs. The bands were not defined entirely by kinship criteria, as no one clan formed a band, but a band was sometimes dominated by its largest clan. The Crow did not have a regular national political system in which band leaders or prominent leaders would gather to discuss pressing issues. Unlike the Northern Cheyenne, the Crow did not have a myth that specified a divine law or political order; most social and political loyalties went to the bands and clans (Lowie 1956:326). Clans were not formal units of a political order, but were instrumental ties for gaining political support.

Crow relations to the supernatural world were highly individualistic, as was typical of many hunting societies (Campbell 1976b, 1988). In order to gain supernatural support and an indication of life goals, the young

Crow sought visions through fasting (Lowie 1956:254; Voget 1980:181). The Creator gave the gift of a vision through intermediary spirits; the Creator was "a pervasive agent, omnipotent over all natural forces, yet part of all natural forces, the ultimate life force, and the perennial meaning of the cosmos" (Frey 1987:63, 77–78). After following the correct ritual, the young warrior was visited by a spirit and experienced a vision indicating whether he should become a warrior, leader, hunter, or shaman. A man who was a skilled hunter or a great warrior was said to have strong spirit helpers. The spirit revealed in the vision – an animal or object – was the vision seeker's instructor and mediator with the cosmic force of the Creator.

Crow extra-band political structure was fluid, and men strove to gain political leadership by gathering the largest following. Political leadership was determined through charisma and personality. Crow men competed for recognition extending beyond their local kinship and band groups in several ways: by acquiring the most powerful spirit helpers, by owning powerful spirit bundles, by redistributing the hunt or spoils in war, by performing acts of bravery and military leadership, and by belonging to one of the warrior societies (Roll 1979:101–102; Frey 1987:21–23).

Crow relations with the United States were accommodating. The Crow did not mount any significant military resistance to the Americans, nor did they take part in the Ghost Dance of the early 1880s, as did many of the other plains nations. Crow leaders saw little purpose in militarily opposing American expansion into the plains, since the Americans were clearly more powerful. The policy of accommodation was legitimated by the dreams and visions of leading Crow political chiefs. In some respects the Crow strategy of accommodation paid off, and the Crow were granted a large tract of land in the 1850s. In subsequent treaties and agreements, in 1868 and 1903, the Crow reservation was reduced to its present size of 2.3 million acres, five times larger than the reservation of the Northern Cheyenne, who gave considerably more direct military resistance to the Americans.

The Crow did not show any strong orientation toward institutionalizing increased societal differentiation before or during the reservation period. They rejected forming a government under the IRA during the 1930s, but were nevertheless subject to American administration of the reservation. In 1941 the Crow adopted the Wind River Shoshone version of the Sun Dance, a ceremony that promotes clan and tribal solidarity (Voget 1980:174–181; Lowie 1956:viii; Jorgensen 1972:177–222). Nevertheless, the influence of Crow ceremonial life and religion on political solidarity remained secondary to kinship and local ties, which predominate in social and political relations (Voget 1981:181).

In 1960 the Crow adopted a constitutional form of government that allowed all adult members the right to constitute the tribal council. A tribal chairman and assistant are elected by majority vote of the assembly. The council meets quarterly to conduct business through a procedure of voting on resolutions. The Crow government might look like a form of direct democracy at first glance, but informal political relations are organized through kinship ties and on some issues through religious groupings (i.e., the Native American Church and various Christian denominations).

Many political leaders and elders take part in local religious activities, such as sweat baths, peyote meetings, the Sun Dance, and the Tobacco Society. Possession of a powerful vision or spirit helpers, gained through purchase, inheritance, or a vision quest, continues to play an important part in social and political prestige. Clan elders often pass on powerful dreams that help assure wealth and political success to their purchasers or inheritors. Political leadership and social prestige, too, are closely associated with the ability to accumulate and redistribute wealth. To attain political office – and to remain in office – you must participate in economic trades with matrilineal kin as a means to repay social and ceremonial obligation (Voget 1981:172-175; 1952:90; Lowie 1956:401; Frey 1987:46-57).

As on many reservations, the tribal government controls most of the political and economic resources, and thus access to jobs and program benefits often depends on political ties. Since no one individual or coalition can control the tribal government, the Crow kin groups and religious groups often form coalitions based on the qualities of individual coalition leaders and on specific political issues. Kinship groups remain central features of Crow social relations and influence political relations: "When an aspirant to a tribal council office is seeking support, his clansmen can be counted on for the money needed for a feed and a political rally and for votes at an election" (Frey 1987:43-44). A primary goal of Crow political coalitions is to control the tribal government by gathering a majority of voters at the quarterly Crow council meetings. A majority coalition can win on all resolutions presented before the council, and can introduce resolutions to impeach the standing tribal leaders, who must either regain the majority before the next quarterly meeting or resign. The political coalitions are shifting and unstable, founded on appeals to individual interests and kin affiliations through promises of access to tribal government jobs, program benefits, and per capita distributions of tribal income.

Oil, Coal, and the Crow

A major change in the Crow economy occurred in the 1970s. The Arab oil embargo and the subsequent rise in the price of oil made eastern Montana an attractive domestic energy source. Like the Northern Cheyenne reservation, much of the Crow reservation had been leased by the BIA to coal mining companies. The Northern Cheyenne, however, had won an annulment of the early contracts because of violations of Department of the Interior regulations. The same ruling that released the Northern Cheyenne from their leases applied to the Crow reservation. In contrast to the Northern Cheyenne, however, the Crow were willing to negotiate contracts for limited strip mining and power plant construction on their reservation (Smith 1982:53–54; Crow Tribal meeting 4/83).

In 1980, the Crow government completed an agreement with Shell Oil Company to strip-mine one 2,560-acre tract. Although the Crow have continued to seek more contracts for coal mining and oil exploration, demand since the late 1970s has declined. The Crow administrations have also been pursuing an oil-drilling merger with a corporate partner, and have studied the feasibility of joint ventures for several 500-megawatt coal-burning electrical generating plants and a synthetic fuel plant on the reservation (Smith 1982:53–54).

The Crow's willingness to participate in coal and energy development contrasts sharply with the vehement rejection expressed by most Northern Cheyenne to strip mining and energy development. Both groups are located in eastern Montana, both have per capita income levels that are less than half the American average, and both have greater than depression-level unemployment rates. The members of both reservations were well informed about the potential benefits and drawbacks of strip mining and energy development (Crow Impact Study Office 1977; Nordstrom et al. 1977:22–23). The Crow, in efforts to protect sacred sites, have tried to localize strip mining to areas where ecological damage will be minimized. Perhaps because the Crow reservation is five times the size of the Northern Cheyenne reservation, the Crow feel that limited strip mining and energy development can be tolerated. However, this argument does not explain the more aggressive development orientation by the Crow, who continue to seek out market-value mineral export agreements, joint ventures, and coal and oil agreements.

This relative willingness to engage in large-scale energy development does not derive from a materialist orientation. Most Crow are poor and are tied into networks of economic and ceremonial reciprocity, and continue to emphasize donations to the needy and to kinfolk over individual wealth. Nevertheless, the dynamics of Crow culture and political and social organization go far in illuminating Crow motives for actively pursuing resource development.

Crow political leadership continues to be determined through charisma and personality. Men who obtain political office must be spiritually authorized and willing to participate in kinship and ceremonial reciprocities. In order to guarantee election, political candidates or sitting leaders must solidify a majority of supporters at every quarterly council meeting, or otherwise face impeachment or political exclusion by rival coalitions. A coalition is held together by kinship ties and obligations, but nonkinsmen need promises of economic reward and benefits extending from the leader's access to tribal resources when in office (Frey 1987:27). One way to increase tribal income is to promise to finalize coal and energy development contracts that include provisions for large per capita payments to tribal members. Consequently, tribal leaders are under great pressure to augment tribal income through energy and natural resource development.

There is something tragic in this pursuit of coal and energy resource development. Despite a willingness to engage in such development, the Crow social order remains primarily decentralized and segmentary, with nondifferentiated relations between polity and community. Consequently, the Crow today are not institutionally positioned to manage coal and energy operations on the reservation. They have no means to affirm hierarchical, bureaucratic, secular, impersonal, nonkin-based, and apolitical economic enterprises within their present institutional order. It is unlikely that Crow institutions will change soon in order to accommodate large-scale resource development.

The Northern Arapahoe

As mentioned earlier, the societies of the plains have often been characterized as being divided between conservatives and "progressives" over issues of accepting American forms of constitutional and representative government. Although the Sioux reservations offer the prime example, the Northern Cheyenne have also experienced internal discord over the IRA form of government, in which elections are often disputed and the council maintains plenary powers over the executive and judiciary branches of the government. The Crow rejected an IRA government and accommodated US demands for political change by adopting a constitutional government that rejected representative government, although it did accept majority rule. Nevertheless, within their constitutional government, the Crow preserved much of their earlier political order based on followings grouped behind charismatic leaders.

The Northern Arapahoe have devised yet another solution to the struggle between reservation life and US demands for institutional and cultural change. According to Fowler (1982a), the Northern Arapahoe have accepted limited change in political organization and have legitimated those changes from within their social and cultural order. Their reservation government enjoys the moral support and commitments of most community members. Because they experienced similar reservation conditions to the other plains nations, the comparative institutional stability of the Northern Arapahoe must derive from their cultural and institutional order. Fowler (1982a) reports that the Northern Arapahoe retained their central symbols of leadership and authority within the reservation framework. Although I will follow Fowler's argument, I will offer a somewhat different, comparative interpretation to that analysis.

Social Organization

The Arapahoe and a kindred nation, the Gros Ventre, have a relatively unique social organization among North American societies. Both societies were organized according to age-grades — systems well known in Africa and other places, but rare in North America. Arapahoe men were divided into seven age-grades, organized as medicine lodges. One advanced through the age-grades after acquiring the ceremonial knowledge necessary to "graduate" into the next medicine lodge. The political leaders of the nation were selected from the sixth-highest lodge, which contained men in their forties and fifties. The seventh, and highest, age-grade was composed of men who were in their sixties and older, who were not active as political leaders, but were the depositories and leaders of the mythology and ceremonies of the nation. They were held in great respect, and their age was a sign of favor from the Creator.

From the seventh lodge were selected seven priests and one Keeper of the Sacred Pipe. The seven priests conducted and led ceremonies, and appointed the men who would be the political leaders in the sixth lodge. The Keeper of the Sacred Pipe cared for the sacred pipe, the embodiment of the covenant relation between the Arapahoe and the Creator. The Creator provided the Arapahoe with sacred laws, morals, and institutional order; as long as the Arapahoe obeyed his laws the people would prosper. The priests and elders of the seventh lodge interpreted the signs and portents from the Creator, and they stood in an intermediary position between the people and the Creator (Fowler 1982a:1–10).

There are several critical aspects that indicate the form of social integration and societal differentiation in Arapahoe society. First, the Arapahoe had a religiously integrated national society, with society-wide ceremonies and ceremonial institutions. Second, the age-grade system took precedence over ties and allegiances to local kinship groups, making kinship a secondary form of social organization and identification. The age-grades integrated men from all localities and kin groups into religiously organized lodges, which were in turn organized into a religiously legitimated order and hierarchy of duties, responsibilities, and functions. Thus the religious integration of Arapahoe society was differentiated from kinship and locality, and had a national institutional form. Third, the religious sphere was superordinate and differentiated from the political sphere. The symbols of authority rested with those in the seventh lodge and were used to regulate the actions of the political leaders in the sixth lodge, who, if they transgressed the religious or moral order, brought misfortune upon the people. By conforming to community consensus and acting in accordance with the religious and moral order, the political leaders of the sixth lodge fulfilled their duties to the nation. The solidarity derived from the institutions of national religious integration and the differentiation of political and religious leadership made the Northern Arapahoe more receptive to limited innovations in political organization.

Like the other plains nations, the Northern Arapahoe had been forced onto a reservation by the 1890s—on the Wind River reservation with a Shoshone band that had been a former enemy. Consequently, both groups have retained considerable self-government even after the formation of a reservation government. Numerous Northern Arapahoe accepted the Ghost Dance, unlike the Crow and most Northern Cheyenne, who did not take up the Ghost Dance in the early 1890s. (One band of Northern Cheyenne that was associated with the Sioux at Pine Ridge adopted the Ghost Dance.) Many Crow and Northern Cheyenne adopted the peyote religion in the early part of the twentieth century. Northern Arapahoe elders taught that the new cults were acceptable as long as they did not interfere with the primary Arapahoe religious beliefs and institutions. The peyote cult has survived among the Northern Arapahoe and today is considered an alternative way of praying (Fowler 1982a:122–125).

The continuity of the religious organization of Northern Arapahoe society appears to have been central to their capacity to retain community solidarity and political-moral order. The Gros Ventre had a similar age-grade system, but their religious leadership was defunct by the second decade of the twentieth century. Without continued ceremonial and religious integration, the Gros Ventre took a different path during their reservation confinement at Fort Belknap in Montana, and accepted an IRA government in the 1930s. Fowler (1982b:74; 1987) does not find a similar community solidarity and political moral order among the contemporary Gros Ventre community and tribal government to what she found among the Northern Arapahoe. Without the ceremonial and religious integration of the age-grades, the Gros Ventre had more difficulties upholding community and political consensus.

Between 1893 and the mid-1930s, the US government attempted to undermine the Arapahoe political leaders by introducing several constitutional reforms. In 1893 a business council was formed to centralize bureaucratic relations with the Arapahoe and make it easier for government officials to transact business through a small number of elected leaders. The Arapahoe, however, while rejecting constitutional reforms and the IRA government, incorporated the business council into their own institutional order. The elders opposed a differentiated constitutional government, knowing that it would depreciate their religious and political authority. Within the context of an elected business council, however, the Arapahoe often merely confirmed through the ballot box those leaders who had been selected by the priests. The elected leaders were inducted into office by the elders. When men who were younger than the sixth age-grade were elected, the religious elders ceremonially authorized the choices. The leaders continued to act as spokesmen for community consensus, rather than as representatives with delegated political powers.

During the 1930s many aspects of the age-grade system fell into disuse, such as the passing of medicine bundles from teachers to apprentices within the lodges. Nevertheless, the elders continued to hold the respect and commitments of the community, and worked to uphold social unity and political consensus (Fowler 1982a:13, 102). The Arapahoe elders favored education, farming, ranching, and other innovations, as long as the people continued to uphold Arapahoe values and norms (Fowler 1982a:175).

After the Arapahoe rejected the IRA government, US officials continued to press for political change. The Arapahoe elders, however, retained their influence; the government continued to be run by the elected business council, which is formally secular from the American point of view, but was regulated by the religious orientations and morals of the elders and by community consensus. Thus the Arapahoe incorporated the business council into their own cultural and institutional framework, and the councilmen acted within the consensual and moral-religious order of Arapahoe society (Fowler 1982a:255). Fowler (1982a:275) argues that the religious-moral organization of Northern Arapahoe society has resulted in relatively stable political relations, free of the factional cleavages, the struggles for political spoils, and the conflicts over representative forms of government that are often reported within other plains nations.

The Northern Arapahoe have reformulated some of their symbols of political authority because of the changes imposed by the early Office of Indian Affairs through the business council and several proposed but rejected constitutional governments. Generally, however, the Arapahoe resisted institutional change, and retained the age-grade hierarchy even after the old buffalo hunting societies were phased out and even after the cultural losses brought on by assimilation during the reservation period prior to 1934.

The capability of the Arapahoe to institutionalize limited political innovations derives from the differentiation of political and religious authority. Because Arapahoe political organization was not directly defined by the age-grade religious system, there was some leeway in adopting political innovations. Compare the Arapahoe to the Northern Cheyenne, for instance. During the reservation period, the Northern Cheyenne retained much of their religious beliefs, but they could not salvage their religiously ordained council of chiefs and soldier societies within the imposed framework of the business council. The Cheyenne chiefs and soldiers continued to manage ceremonies, such as the Sun Dance, but they were increasingly excluded from the secular political sphere. In the Arapahoe case, the religious authority of the seventh lodge was not specific to or contingent on political organization, and the priests sanctioned political leadership within the business council as they had done for the leaders among the earlier bands. Under the pressures of the reservation period, the less-differentiated and less–socially integrated Cheyenne political-religious system disintegrated. In comparison, the Arapahoe age-grades were more congruent with American secular political organization, and the Arapahoe were thus less pressed to make major changes in political and religious relations.

Social Change on the Plains

The plains nations are often described in terms of their cultural, political, and social disintegration after the loss of the buffalo hunt and restriction to reservations. In the cases described here, however, the institutional responses to the reservation system vary considerably. Some of the Sioux reservations, such as Pine Ridge, Rosebud, and Crow Creek, show limited institutionalization of representative and differentiated forms of government, a result of the conflicting cultural-normative orders associated with local, kin-based political authority that has little congruence with the norms of representative government. Several Sioux reservations continue to experience internal conflict over the rules of organization of the polity. The Sioux, with their kin-based and decentralized social and political order, have found it difficult to consensually institutionalize political centralization, political secularization, and the differentiation of polity and kinship, some of the political innovations introduced and upheld by BIA.

The Northern Cheyenne, Crow, and Northern Arapahoe have adapted to American demands for political change and to the conditions of the reservation environment by accepting more stable political forms. The Northern Cheyenne IRA government was the least normatively institutionalized. The chief and warrior societies were progressively excluded from the early business council and from the later IRA government. In Northern Cheyenne society, the religious sphere rules over the political sphere, and its survival has derived largely from religious and community commitments to cultural and political survival. The Northern Cheyenne polity has become more secular under the IRA government and subject to BIA regulations, and often the political sphere appears unstable as extended families contend for political leadership. Nonetheless, Northern Cheyenne cultural stability, community consensus, and primary value orientations toward tribal survival derive from the religiously integrated tribal community.

Both the Crow and the Northern Arapahoe have rejected IRA governments but have accepted political change that could be incorporated within their own institutional frameworks. Despite the appearance of conflict and chaotic political activity, the Crow government must be considered institutionally stable. The Crow accepted a constitutional government in 1960 that avoided representational government and allowed direct participation by all adults. Thus the Crow did not separate the polity from the community, one of the purposes of representational governments. Within this framework, the Crow have retained many of their traditional political institutions, such as charismatic leadership, informal matrilineal kinship political support, and the informal influence of elders. The Northern Arapahoe have institutionalized their elective council, which according to Fowler enjoys the support and participation of the community. The religiously integrated age-grade system allowed the Arapahoe to express limited acceptance of American-induced political change.

Chapter 5

The Navajo and Quechan in the Southwest

THE SOUTHWEST PAINTS a complex picture in terms of its ecology, geopolitical relations, and variety of societal forms. From the 1540s until the year 1821 the primary colonial power in the area was Spain, for whom the area in present-day Arizona, New Mexico, and southern California was a peripheral and generally unimportant province. The southwest came under brief Mexican control from 1821 until American conquest in 1846–1848 and its consolidation into the United States during the 1850s (Hall 1989). The region was populated by a variety of indigenous societies, such as the Hopi, Papagos, and Quechan, numerous pueblo villages along the Rio Grande, and Athapascan groups such as the Navajo and Apache. The Athapascans were relatively recent immigrants, having come into the area sometime after 1300 A.D. Primarily hunting and gathering societies, the Athapascans soon adopted and assimilated selected aspects of the culture, ceremonies, and world views of the horticultural pueblo peoples.

The Navajo and Quechan provide examples of social change in the southwest. The Navajo were an Athapascan immigrant group that has become the most populous Indian tribe in the United States today. They currently occupy a large reservation that extends into both Arizona and New Mexico and surrounds the Hopi reservation. The Quechan, or Yuma, are a nonpueblo group currently located on a reservation on the southern California–Arizona border. They occupied this area for an extended period, most likely before the arrival of the Navajo. Both societies were politically decentralized, with kin-based political orders. During the twentieth century, the Navajo rejected adoption of an IRA government, instead gradually adopting a differentiated tribal government, and the Quechan adopted an IRA government. Although both groups experienced difficulties institutionalizing the new political forms, the Navajo government appears to be more extensively organized and stable than the Quechan government.

The Quechan

This section reinterprets the historical work of Bee (1963, 1981) on the Quechan. The early Quechan did not have a regular or centralized political structure; their political loyalties were committed to local kinship groups. Their basic political, social, and economic units were settlements composed of extended families. The kinship groups appear to have been exogamous, patrilineal clans. Each settlement was politically dominated by one clan, although often more than one clan lived in a settlement. Settlement and kinship loyalties took precedence over loyalties to the tribal group (Bee 1963:209), making social and political solidarity local and decentralized.

The Quechan formed regular extralocal relations in both religious and military affairs. Settlement and kinship affiliations were not recognized in military organization; instead, warrior and war leadership roles were allocated according to skill and gender. Military organization was the most unified Quechan institution; it mobilized all the settlements into a fighting force against nearby Indian tribes and against early Spanish and American intruders. The Quechan practiced society-wide religious mourning ceremonies, but Quechan religion and ceremonial culture did not demand more than occasional gatherings. They shared religious beliefs, but religious experiences were often personal, taking the form of dreams or visions that were interpreted by the elders and provided indications of future life roles or goals. The annual tribal ceremonies did not translate into greater political solidarity; the local settlements remained politically, socially, and economically segmented groups.

The qualifications for political leadership within the settlement depended on speaking ability, competence, generosity, and validation through special dreams. The right dream or vision was one in which a ladder extended down from heaven and the man was invited to ascend. If he ascended and returned, then he was approved for a leadership role. If he declined to ascend the ladder, then he was disqualified from consideration. The candidates told the dreams to the elders, who interpreted them. A man who had the proper dreams and who could speak well might command a following or persuade a majority to his opinion on a specific issue. Succession in leadership was not hereditary, but leaders did tend to come from certain families as long as they were competent men who had the proper dreams or visions (Bee 1981:9–10). The settlement leaders did not command coercive powers and did not control significant political or economic resources. Political decision-making was based on negotiation and consensus among the settlement members. Thus, Quechan political leadership was localistic, charismatic, and without coercive powers.

The Quechan organized early military resistance to American intrusions, but after a defeat in 1852, they did not organize any more sustained collective resistance before being moved to a reservation in 1884. They did not respond to increasing American hegemony with a revitalization movement or by institutionalizing increased political cohesiveness or political centralization; their social and political organization remained decentralized and segmentary. In the 1880s there were six independent settlement groups; each had its own headman, and there was little political consensus among the six primary leaders (Bee 1981:21–23). Quechan leaders increasingly were appointed by US officials, a situation that engendered opposition from conservative Quechan. Factionalism erupted over the legitimacy of American-appointed leaders, over whether to accept American schools, and over the pros and cons of ceding land to the United States. The last issue further diminished Quechan social and political cohesiveness, which was already decentralized and segmentary. These disputes reduced the possibilities and effectiveness of the Quechan to challenge or negotiate American polices (Bee 1981:46).

After a 45,000-acre reservation was established in 1884, Quechan internal factionalism and disunity was exploited by US officials (Bee 1981:62), and between 1912 and 1914 American agents divided and allotted land on the Quechan reservation. Much of the most marginal land was assigned to the Quechan, and fertile land was made available to American farmers. Because of the strength of American bureaucratic control over reservation resources and institutions and the absence of sustained collective unity, the Quechan were unable to oppose this misuse of their land.

With little apparent enthusiasm, the Quechan ratified an IRA constitution in 1936. The new tribal council enjoyed little community support; few Quechan voted in tribal elections during the 1930s, 1940s, and even into the 1950s (Bee 1981:96–99). During this period the settlements began to break into smaller, more numerous groups. The IRA government did not lead to greater social or political solidarity among the Quechan, since many avoided actively participating in it.

Prior to the 1960s, the tribal government had commanded limited resources and came under strict BIA financial and administrative control.

Then, significant financial and organizational resources became available to the Quechan government during the antipoverty programs of the 1960s, and these allowed the tribal government to more directly control funds and programs. The tribal government became a major center for jobs and program benefits on the reservation, and political competition intensified for access to those favors and to political office. Despite enhanced tribal control over jobs, money, and administrative organization and an improved bargaining position against the BIA, Quechan factionalism and political conflict persisted (Bee 1981:157). The influx of material resources and local control over these resources only intensified the already decentralized factions and social-political cleavages.

Throughout the reservation period, kinship groups remained the most important Quechan economic, social, and political groups (Bee 1981:163). Attempts to impose a unified political system through the IRA government or to enhance community resources through antipoverty programs did not lead to greater Quechan political solidarity. The presence of frequent external threats of economic exploitation and political domination also failed to provide a basis for promoting sustained political unity. During the 1940s and 1950s there were only occasional incidents of united opposition against US policies, and the 1960s saw only a few protest movements against violations of Quechan political sovereignty. All these movements were brief; Quechan kin groups and factions would unite temporarily, and then dissolve soon after the passing of the crisis.

The Quechan example suggests that societies with cultural orders that do not legitimate society-wide social or political commitments will find it difficult to mobilize sustained collective action to protect their interests. They will have difficulty institutionalizing significant changes in political centralization and differentiation, despite access to resources, American threats to political autonomy and land, and even externally imposed attempts to build a more unified, centralized, and differentiated political order. Furthermore, such a decentralized social and political order tends to exacerbate the negative effects of colonial domination by weakening the possibilities of sustained collective opposition.

The Navajo

The Navajo were an Athapascan-speaking nation of hunters and gatherers. They appear to have had relatively little contact with the Spanish prior to 1700. By the late 1600s, the Navajo had begun to farm, although they were still more engaged in hunting and gathering than were the Rio Grande pueblos. After the revolt by the eastern pueblos in the 1680 and the subsequent Spanish reconquest in 1696, many members of the Jemez, Tewa, and Keresan pueblos joined Navajo bands. The pueblos intermarried with the Navajo and introduced cultural and technical innovations into Navajo society. The Navajo culture and language remained preeminent in the mixed groups, but the Navajo assimilated many aspects of the pueblo horticultural world view into their own mythology. During the 1700s the Navajo bands were located between the Hopi villages and the eastern pueblo villages, much the same territory that they occupy today. They took up farming more seriously and also adopted domestic animals such as sheep and horses, which they periodically acquired by raiding Spanish and pueblo settlements (Spicer 1962:211–213). Throughout the Spanish and Mexican periods, up until the 1850s, the Navajo enjoyed independence from colonial political, administrative, and mission controls. In contrast, the eastern pueblos on the Rio Grande had early on – by the late 1590s – felt the brunt of Spanish administration and missionaries.

Between 1846 and 1863 the US Army undertook the task of subduing the Navajo. After numerous campaigns, the army gathered about 8,000 Navajo and transported them to captivity at Bosque Redondo in 1864. For four years the Navajo were kept in captivity – their first experience in colonial domination and their first sustained contact with the Americans. Several thousand Navajo died, many from disease. In 1868 the Navajo agreed to a treaty establishing a reservation of about one-quarter of their former territory, and they were released to walk the 300 miles to their reservation (Spicer 1962:220–221). Today the Navajo occupy four reservations, three in New Mexico and another, the large Navajo Reservation, which straddles the Arizona–New Mexico border.

During captivity the Americans treated the Navajo as a single national unit, and even recognized a central leader and assistant chiefs. When the Navajo were released the centralized proto-tribal organization was continued, but by the 1890s the Navajo had decentralized toward their former band and kin-based local organization, which emphasized local group autonomy and leadership. The Navajo returned to sheep and goat herding, and for some time many did not recognize the boundaries of the new reservation, preferring instead to use the land as they had done previously.

By the end of the nineteenth century the Navajo had already adopted economic institutions and techniques from the Pueblo and Spanish. Many were sheep herders, and some had extensive herds, although most Navajo engaged in sheep herding primarily for subsistence needs, trading limited surpluses at local trade posts. Despite American attempts to recognize and encourage a more centralized political organization, the Navajo remained socially, economically, and politically organized in local land-use groups composed of clan, domestic, and genealogical kinship affiliations (Spicer

1962:228; Lamphere 1977:30–31; Williams 1970:36–37). The bands ranged from 10 to 40 extended families each of which occupied between one and ten hogans (dwellings). There is some indication that the local Navajo bands were formed into a symbolic or ceremonial hierarchy, in which they gathered and discussed issues of war and peace. In the 1840s there were reports of 12 peace chiefs and 12 war chiefs, who camped in a cosmologically ordered assembly (war chiefs to the north, peace chiefs to the south) with a ceremonial hogan at the center and a chief who served as conductor of ceremonies (Williams 1970:4–5; Young 1978:20–24). All Navajo hogans are symbolic representations of the cosmic universe. They always have eight sides, and the door faces the east toward the rising sun. The dome roof symbolizes the opening of heaven's door, and the fireplace symbolizes the center of the world (Campbell 1988:249). The information on Navajo political order from the nineteenth century is vague, however, and such ceremonial organization does not seem to have survived into the twentieth century.

Each of the local bands had a leader called Naatanii who led the negotiations and consensus forming among the adult members. The band leader administered justice, which consisted primarily of attempting to reestablish harmonious relations between individuals or kinship groups. The headman and his assistants planned and organized farming and stockraising and supervised harvesting, training, and planting of crops. "The reputation of local headmen depended upon his good judgment and his rhetorical ability to persuade members of his group to lead peaceful, useful and harmonious lives" (Williams 1970:7; Young 1978:23).

Leaders were often older men who knew how to perform one or more songs or ritual ceremonies for reestablishing harmonious relations. If a leader or members of his immediate family became ill, died, or suffered an accident, the leader temporarily stepped aside to perform rituals that were intended to return health to his family. If a series of misfortunes occurred, the leader stepped down; bad luck was considered the result of transgressions against the Navajo religious and moral order, or it could mean that the headman had become the target of witchcraft from members of the community who were dissatisfied with his ministry (Williams 1970:16; Young 1978:25–27).

Navajo culture, shamanism, and religion continued to flourish in a strict world view that nested human moral order within a religiously cosmologized order. The human and institutional world was part of the cosmic and mythical order; if humans disturbed the relations of order in nature, in religious relations, or in social institutions, then the Navajo would suffer this-worldly misfortune, such as poverty or disease. To commit a ritual transgression required a ceremony, and often the help of a shaman, to reestablish ritual order.

> It is important to know that the central Navajo's religious ideas are concerned with health and order. . . . Moreover, the kind of order conceived of is primarily of ritual order, that is, order imposed by human religious action, and, for the Navajo this is largely a matter of creating and maintaining health. Health, on its part, is seen as stretching far beyond the individual: it concerns his whole people as well as himself, and is based in large part on a reciprocal relationship with the world of nature, mediated through ritual. The world is seen as an essentially ordered place. (Tolkein 1969:229)

The Navajo shared a common world view that involved a complex of myths and ritual that applied to everyday life and demanded individual motivation toward maintaining ritual harmony among the natural, social, and supernatural orders. This orientation resembles the world view of the southeastern nations, and should orient the social action of well-socialized Navajo toward conservatism and opposition to social, economic, religious, or political innovations that might threaten the balance within the ritual order of the universe.

Forming the Navajo Tribal Government

Most of the initiative for building a more centralized Navajo political structure did not come from the Navajo, but rather from US officials. The American efforts were always resisted by the local leaders, who often did not recognize and were not willing to participate in the early American suggestions for a more centralized government. The Americans had recognized certain Navajo leaders after 1868, but they received little recognition from the local Navajo leaders, who nevertheless acquiesced to American demands. Between 1868 and 1936 the American-recognized Navajo leaders did not gain the support and commitment of the local leaders.

In 1921, US officials on the Navajo reservation were assembling the large number of headmen and people to manage Navajo business and bureaucratic issues. After the discovery of oil, these officials considered the large assembly inadequate to manage the business concerns of oil and resource development. In 1922 several oil leases were negotiated with a group of local headmen, but the leases were rejected by the Department of the Interior under the reasoning that a small group of headmen were not collectively invested with the right to negotiate leases for the Navajo nation. According to the treaty of 1868, three-fourths of the Navajo Nation had to favor a mineral lease before a contract could be considered valid. Getting such agreement from the Navajo was difficult, and so American officials moved to create a business council that would have the power to negotiate contracts for the Navajo nation.

In January 1923, the commissioner of Indian affairs issued regulations for the formation of a business council with the legal authority to approve leasing contracts (Young 1978:59). In April, the reservation superintendent called together several leaders and invited the men to form a business committee. The business council consisted of 12 elected members, 12 alternates, and the tribal chairman and vice chairman, who were elected at large for four-year terms. The delegates organized themselves into the first elected body, and signed gas and oil leases that were legally binding for the entire Navajo nation. In 1928 women were given the right to vote, and in 1934 the council was extended to 24 members and the alternates were eliminated (Williams 1970:19-23).

During that same period, several reservation superintendents attempted to organize local chapters among the Navajo. American officials saw the chapters as a means to create better communication between Navajo communities and the US government, to promote local self-help programs and to create a political organization for expressing opinions about government programs and policies. Prior to the 1950s the chapters were not formally linked to the central tribal government, although after 1936 the chapters became precincts under the reorganized council. The US plan for the local chapter organizations resembled that of a voluntary association wherein the principles of elected representative leadership, majority rule, right of women to vote, and parliamentary procedures would prevail. By 1928 there were five organized chapters; each built a meeting house, made roads, and worked on irrigation and community water works. During the 1930s chapters were organized in many locations on the reservation, and were known as Livestock Associations or Farming Associations.

Instead of the town meeting model introduced by the Americans, however, the chapters adhered largely to the norms and leadership of the traditional local leaders. Community consensus, kinship, clan ties, and emphasis on maintaining harmonious relations prevailed. Generally the local headman was elected president of the chapter, and the meetings were conducted according to the rules requiring community consensus and through the dynamics of matrilineal kin relations rather than parliamentary procedures. By 1937 there were 80 organized chapters, most of which were engaged in community improvement projects (Williams 1970:35-38; Young 1978:66-67).

A major conflict erupted between the US government and the Navajo nation in the 1930s. US officials argued that the Navajo herders were overgrazing their land base and demanded that they substantially reduce their horse and sheep herds. Since many Navajo were subsistence sheep herders, they were reluctant to cut back while the more wealthy herders used their business and English skills to lobby the government and gain agreements that limited their losses. Thus the demands for herd reduction fell disproportionately to the subsistence herders, who were strongly resistant to American interference into their economic affairs. Many local leaders used the chapters to mobilize resistance against American demands. Recognizing this, the Americans withdrew their support for the chapters. Without direct American support the chapters dwindled, and by 1943 only 40 remained. Most communities then returned to their traditional form of local political organization. The chapters were revived by the Navajo tribal government in the 1950s (Williams 1970:37–38, 40).

Between 1923 and 1936 the business committee gained little local support or legitimacy among most Navajo. Most Navajo ignored the central political system organized by American officials and led by wealthy stockmen, who were more familiar with American political culture than most subsistence oriented Navajo. In June 1935, at least partly due to the stock reduction controversy, Navajo voters rejected the proposal of an IRA constitutional government by a vote of 7,992 to 7,608.

In 1936 the Navajo Business Council gave approval to American policies, which demanded stock reductions, but the chapters and local communities rejected the decision (Williams 1970:60). From the Navajo point of view, the elected leaders were supposed to participate in ceremonies designed to sanctify major decisions and to represent the consensus and will of the local communities. The business council, devoid of authority, was dissolved; it had never had executive or legislative powers and could not act without the approval of BIA.

With the permission of the secretary of the interior, the Navajo agreed to reorganize their government. American officials held that a constitutional government that included the local headmen would bring the Navajo into conformity with American stock reduction regulations. In early April 1937 a committee on reorganization was formed by 170 Navajo delegates; a draft constitution was forwarded to the secretary of the interior in October. The proposed constitution, which repealed federal regulation over Navajo political and government affairs, did not receive the secretary's approval (Young 1978:108). Instead he issued "Rules for the Navajo Council," or, as they are often called, the "Rules of 1938," under which the US government retained considerable regulatory powers over the Navajo government (Young 1978:114–118).

The new tribal government had 74 elected representatives and operated much like the IRA governments. The tribal chairman, vice chairman, and delegates were elected every four years. Conflict continued between Navajo communities and the US-backed government over the policies of American-directed change and stock reductions. Furthermore, the Americans and the Navajo did not share opinions regarding the role, purpose, function, and authority of the new Navajo government. Active opposition to stock reduction and to what was considered nonlegitimate centralized authority of the Navajo tribal council continued into the 1940s and 1950s, abating somewhat during the 1960s (Spicer 1962:228; Williams 1970:60–62).

In 1955 the secretary of the interior decided to allow the chapters to become a part of the Navajo tribal government. Although the number of active chapters had been reduced to 40, the new direction of incorporating the local communities into the Navajo government led to the revival of many. By 1960 92 chapters were operating throughout the reservation. The local chapters are now part of the tribal government organization, but they do not operate on the New England town meeting model that the American initiators intended. The chapters have been popular because they can be organized according to the traditional leadership patterns and norms of the local land use group. Chapter leaders are required to exercise traditional leadership qualities; they must have exemplary character, good speaking skills, personal charisma, proven ability in practical matters, and knowledge of conducting sings and ceremonies, and they must not make decisions without community consensus (Lamphere 1977:30).

Although the organization of the Navajo chapters in formal voluntary associations would seem to imply, from the Western point of view, direct individual participation and political commitments to the chapter organization, the chapters do not command primary Navajo political loyalties. Rural Navajo political identification continues to be with clan affiliations, genealogical kinship ties, and the local land use community group (Lamphere 1977:30; Williams 1970:62 ff). Navajo community social and political norms predominate in the chapter organizations, and it seems doubtful that they can be the basis for authorizing and institutionalizing the centralized Navajo tribal government.

More recently it has been argued that the Navajo have formed an increasing sense of nationalism, which in turn has led to a more centralized, differentiated, and legitimate Navajo tribal government. This nationalism comes from a variety of sources: more Navajo professionals, businesspeople, and wage laborers, increased financial resources from mineral sales, direct legal and political competition from surrounding states and the federal government, and American policies and bureaucracy, which treat the Navajo as a collective group (Iverson 1981:xxiii, 10, 74; Shepardson 1963:113; 1965:250–253). Although the Navajo government fulfills a role that is imposed by changing political and economic relations with the United States, Navajo social and political normative order remains local and kin based. Thus the normative support for the more centralized and differentiated Navajo government still remains tenuous. This argument can be seen in the process by which the Navajo formed an independent judiciary.

In 1959 the Navajo tribal council accepted full responsibility for administering law and order on the reservation. The council felt that it was forced to adopt an American court system, convinced that failure to do so would invite the surrounding states of New Mexico and Arizona to impose their laws and courts on the Navajo. The motivation to create a court system, then, did not arise from Navajo values or ideals, but from the need to prevent external threats. The American court system did not share a common sense of justice with the local communities, which traditionally dispensed justice through local leaders and community consensus.

Nevertheless, the Navajo have adopted the court system and they do participate in its sessions. The courts have replaced the local headmen and chapter officers, thereby constituting a further differentiation of polity from judicial relations within Navajo society. The Navajo use the courts under certain conditions. Conservative Navajo use the courts when the proceedings can be conducted in the traditional manner of conflict resolution: the judge is required to mediate a dispute and supply a judgment that will restore harmony and consensus. Conservative Navajo also use the courts when the law of the court conflicts with Navajo customary laws and norms — for example, when a medicine bundle is inherited by children of the deceased rather than by someone who has the sacred knowledge to properly use the bundle. Cases of drunkenness are considered to be more effectively handled by the courts and police rather than by traditional means of social control (Shepardson 1965:253).

Under American pressure in the early 1970s to reorganize the chapter system in order to create a more equitable distribution of tribal council representatives to population, the council attempted to restructure the boundaries of the chapters. Some chapters had one council member for fewer than 500 members, and the largest chapter had nearly 7,000 members but only one council representative. Many communities were reluctant to adopt the change, considering it a direct attempt by the council to weaken the influence of the traditional headmen and their communities. By 1978 the Navajo court system had heard 36 boundary disputes among 102 chapters. The reassignment of representatives to the unicameral tribal council by population, however, did not change the basic relation of the chapters to the central government. Each chapter retained direct access to the central government, but now some chapters with larger populations had more representatives in an 87-member council. The realignment preserved local political traditions within the structure of the council and chapter system (Iverson 1981:201–211).

In recent years some Navajo have focused on building national allegiances over local and kinship loyalties, believing that only a unified tribal government will preserve Navajo lands and resources. Under these conditions Navajo nationalism is largely a mutual pact of resistance against potentially coercive external forces, but Navajo nationalism is not necessarily legitimatized by the decentralized, segmentary, kin-based, local groupings that compose Navajo society. Nevertheless, the Navajo tribal council holds regular elections and court sessions, and governs the most populous Indian group in the United States. The main forces of Navajo nationalism have come from external political, economic, and bureaucratic competition; it is not entirely clear that the tribal government has been fully institutionalized through the commitments and support of the local communities. Nevertheless, incorporating local communities into the tribal government structure is one of the most extensive attempts by a tribal government to integrate a decentralized and particularistically organized community into a centralized, differentiated tribal government. The local communities have generally resisted centralization while readily adopting the chapter organizational form because the local communities could operate the chapters by means of their own understandings of political order. The central government, however, was organized according to American principles, which the members of the local communities have often thought were too autocratic, too secular, and often contrary to the interests of the communities.

The Navajo and Quechan: A Comparison

Both the Navajo and Quechan had decentralized social and political institutions in which kinship and local political relations were not differentiated. Both groups showed considerable resistance to political centralization and increased political differentiation. The Navajo, due to their large population — at least 167,000 — and their rich endowment of raw materials, received considerable attention and pressure for change from American officials. Most political innovations toward centralization and differentiation were introduced into Navajo society by Americans. Left to themselves, it is doubtful that the Navajo would have followed a similar path. They presently have a differentiated government, which continues to negotiate its legitimacy with the conservative local communities.

Chapter 6

The Tlingit in the Pacific Northwest

T HE PACIFIC NORTHWEST, an ecological zone abundant with fish and wildlife, provided an economic base for a variety of complex cultures. The cultures located in this region, which extends from the Alaska panhandle down to northern California, share a variety of cultural orientations and institutional complexes. The most readily apparent feature is the potlatch, or "giveaway," in which wealth is accumulated and distributed in public displays. Giveaways are prominent in many other North American societies — among the Northern Cheyenne and other plains nations, for example. This emphasis on accumulation of wealth has gained the attention of many scholars, who proffer something of an analogy to the acquisitive emphasis in Western societies. These orientations toward accumulating wealth early on attracted many of the northwesterners into trade and market relations with Westerners (Drucker 1965:211–214). Oftentimes, however, the primary purpose of the potlatch was not economic reinvestment, as is the case with market-oriented, rational capitalist entrepreneurship, but to enhance social status, honor ancestors, or seal marriage agreements. The potlatch should be understood from within its own cultural and institutional framework, and not be too easily compared with self-interested materialism.

The institutional relations within which the potlatch is embedded vary from case to case. The potlatch among the Tlingit, for example, is primarily associated with events initiated by funerals; among the Kwakiutl the potlatch is used to validate the marriage arrangements of the firstborn (Sequin 1985; Rosman and Rubel 1972). Similarly, the northwest coast nations share a common mythological tradition in which the trickster figure Raven is a central character; in the southwest, a similar trickster figure is known as Coyote. The belief in rebirth is predominant in the northwest, but the visions of cosmological order vary from society to society. For example, in the cosmological view of the Bella Coola of present-day British Columbia, the remembered dead occupy the first realm below the earth; they are reborn, but those that are not remembered are relegated to the second realm below the earth and their spirits are lost (Campbell 1988:199). The Tlingit believe that the dead travel to an other-worldly house, although some spirits might perish on the way; from this house, some spirits may be recalled to rebirth within the same clan as their earlier existences.

Just as views of the cosmos and the potlatch vary in the northwest, so does social organization. The Tlingit were organized by two moieties with about 25 clans in each division. They lived in the Alaska panhandle, the northernmost region of the northwest culture area, and as one proceeds south the forms of kinship and social organization range toward more decentralized and segmentary forms. Finally, to add yet another dimension of complexity to the diversity of the Pacific Northwest, the region is currently divided into three geopolitical zones. Most groups in the lower 48 states ("the lower 48"), in present-day Washington, Oregon, and northern California, were subdued and placed on reservations prior to the end of the nineteenth century, and therefore suffered early administrative and economic restrictions. The groups in present-day British Columbia came under the administration of the Canadian government, which in some ways was more direct and restrictive than the American system. The third group of cases are the Tlingit, and parts of the Tsimshian and Haida, who are located in southeast Alaska. The Alaskans were not forced onto reservations and their administration has been indirect compared to the rest of the American- and Canadian- administered northwestern groups. Alaska was a territory from 1867 to 1960, and only a few small reservations were established there. The remainder of the Alaska natives were held in an ambiguous and relatively undefined relation to the US government up until the early 1970s. The Tlingit in Alaska, then, found themselves under less direct colonial administration than the other northwestern culture societies.

The example to be proffered here of social change in the northwest region will be the Tlingit, with reference to the associated Tsimshian and Haida segments located in Alaska. These groups have formed a remarkable institutional response to American contact during the twentieth century. They have enhanced their social unity by revising the potlatch ceremonies to make them reciprocal between the two major moieties. They have centralized and differentiated their political relations by forming the Alaska Native Brotherhood and have accepted further changes in political and economic differentiation by adopting the Tlingit-Haida Central Council in the 1960s and forming the Sealaska Corporation in the 1970s.

The Tlingit

Tlingit social organization was decentralized and segmentary. It had no society-wide political center, and political and social loyalties went to kinship groups and villages. These organizational features would not indicate the likelihood of the subsequent centralization and differentiation in social and political organization. Nevertheless, Tlingit society was integrated by the potlatch ceremony, which was carried on by reciprocal arrangements between clan segments from two opposite moieties. In addition, Tlingit culture supported a hierarchical social order, encouraged competition for social status, and emphasized the accumulation of wealth. All of these features have some congruence with Western societies, and therefore may have eased Tlingit adaptations to American society. But, as will be argued, Tlingit social and political centralization and differentiation cannot be understood as a result deriving from the characteristics of internal institutional and cultural order. The political and economic conditions of contact and the interpenetration of Western values played a central role in explaining the increased social and political solidarity and increased economic and political differentiation of Tlingit society during the twentieth century.

Tlingit society was divided into two moieties, usually named Eagle and Raven. Sometimes in the northern villages the two moieties were called, respectively, Wolf and Bear, but during the twentieth century the emphasis has been on Eagle and Raven, names that are congruent with similar moieties among the Tsimshian and Haida, with whom the Tlingit were in close association and wished to join in social and political activities. Each moiety has about 25 matrilineal clans. Members of the Raven moiety must marry members of the Eagle moiety, although during the present century the strictness of this rule has lapsed. Nevertheless, it is still possible to find young men who will only marry women from the opposite moiety in order not to shame or embarrass their parents.

Each clan is further subdivided into clan segments, which were located in 14 different villages in the Tlingit country. A clan may have segments in one or several villages, but no clan had segments in all villages. The primary political and social loyalties were given to the clan segment, or house. The clan segment occupied a separate communal house, which was further divided into lineages with rank order within the house. The villages were not corporately organized, although the highest-ranked man within the highest-ranked house was the headman of the village. However, his authority was nominal, because the headmen of the houses in the village managed their own affairs. The village government was composed of the headmen of the houses. There was no regular political authority above the houses or villages, and each house was sovereign and derived its rank order from its past prestige in giving goods away in the potlatch.

The Tlingit houses had rights to territory, and to fishing on certain rivers, and each owned ceremonial equipment, a house, a store of songs, dances, music, and mythological tales. The leader of the house managed the house estate, a job that included augmenting the wealth of the house and sponsoring potlatches that enhanced its prestige. The house headman was usually the immediate nephew of the previous headman, although the position was not necessarily hereditary. The leading positions were generally determined by the aristocratic lineages within the house, those who could trace their ancestry most directly to the mythical founders of the house or clan. The farther one's lineage was from the central mythical lineage, the less prestige and rank was conferred. At least during the more intensely competitive contact period, the ability of a leader to produce wealth and enhance the social prestige of the house was a more important criterion for leadership than was birth in a high lineage.

Since house social rank depended on the leadership and acquisitive abilities of the house leader, the failure to appoint their most capable men to leadership positions could easily result in the decline of prestige and rank of the house. Rank order was maintained through community evaluation of the worth of one's potlatches, which required extensive accumulation and giveaway of material goods. Houses were openly competitive in acquiring and displaying wealth, dances, and songs, since the potlatch was the primary means of status mobility in Tlingit society (Swanton 1908:435). House members were bound to contribute to the wealth of the house in order to advance its status. Houses were assigned rank according to their performance at potlatches, and individual house members were accorded rank according to the level of involvement in and contributions made to the potlatch material reciprocities and ceremonies (Olsen 1967:37–48; Krause 1956).

Although potlatches determined the rank order of the houses, individuals received unique potlatch names or titles that designated their in-house rank — aristocrat, commoner or slave. Slaves, usually captured enemies and bastard children, received little status and were sometimes ceremonially executed and placed under the corners of a house during ceremonies. When slaves died they were often left to rot on the beaches, without any ceremony or recognition of interment. The titles of aristocrats and commoners graded into one another, and, as was already mentioned, there were advancement opportunities for ambitious individuals.

This extensive rank order reflected the Tlingit belief in rebirth. The bodies of the dead were cremated, and care was taken that the body was not mutilated, as a disfigurement might reappear on the deceased upon rebirth. The spirits of the dead dwelled in an other-worldly house. According to some versions the spirits required the gifts of the potlatch to keep them comfortable, but other versions claimed that the potlatch gifts were not needed for comfort, but to indicate honor and respect from living clan members. Those who were reborn reappeared again in one of the lineages of the same clan. The goal within this round of rebirths was to be reborn in a wealthy, aristocratic lineage. Those in the highest lineages were those who had effectively performed their clan and house responsibilities in previous lives. Thus the Tlingit world view justified the rank order of Tlingit society. By fulfilling one's clan obligations, submitting to the will of the collective house group, and contributing to potlatches, one could possibly be reborn into a higher-ranked lineage (Krause 1956:193; Stevenson 1966:231–234; Oberg 1960:290–295).

In contrast to the Hindu belief in rebirth, Tlingit beliefs were life affirming. The purpose of the round of rebirths was not to escape the neverending wheel of life, but to enhance this-worldly rank, especially if one was dissatisfied with one's current worldly situation. For the Hindu, conforming to the social order and carrying out the dharma, or obligations of the moral-cosmic order, were focused on eventual escape from the wheel of rebirth into the realm of the gods. For the Tlingit, rebirth opened opportunities for social mobility and escape from lowly social rank.

The potlatch was the central institution of Tlingit social integration. The round of potlatch reciprocities was initiated by the death of a member of one of the houses. The members of the house and moiety of the deceased did not handle the body or funeral arrangements; these duties were carried out by the house and relatives of the spouse of the deceased, who were members of the opposite moiety. The spouse's house and relatives prepared the body for cremation and provided material and social comforts for the bereaved. The potlatch, then, was a way to pay back the members of the spouse's house, who had comforted the bereaved during their time of sorrow. If the deceased was of no special rank, then a return potlatch at some future date would settle the matter and end the period of mourning. If the deceased was the headman of the house, however, an elaborate sequence of ceremonies was initiated in order to establish the next head of the house with appropriate rank. Such activities might include building a new house, raising new totem poles, and granting new titles for those to be honored with higher ranks. These activities took place between the time of the funeral and the repayment during the potlatch. Those who contributed most to the funeral expenses and provided skills and artistic workmanship for the totem pole raising or the house building, were rewarded in the potlatch according to their contributions (Olsen 1967:16; Salisbury 1962:43; Billman 1969:55–64).

The potlatch, however, was more than an exchange of goods and services. The cultural justification for the potlatch was that it was a ceremony intended to honor the clan ancestors. By giving away a large amount of accumulated wealth the bereaved house was not only repaying for services rendered, but it was believed that the spirit of the donated goods went to benefit or honor clan ancestors (Swanton 1908:343, 462–463; Averkieva 1971:331; de Laguna 1954:185–191). The more wealth given away, the more the house rose in community prestige for loving and honoring its clan ancestors. During the potlatch ceremonies, the deceased members of the house and clan are remembered, and their formal names are called out. Among the Bella Coola only those individuals who are remembered are reborn; I have not been able to find a similar belief among the Tlingit, however.

At the time of early contact with Westerners, the Tlingit were politically decentralized and their polity and kinship organization were not differentiated. Tlingit mythology gave legitimacy to particularistic identities among the clans and houses, since each clan had its own origin myth. Even in the potlatch, at this early time, the reciprocal obligations were carried out between houses related by marriage; the clan and moiety were only symbolically entered into these obligations, meaning that the integrative effects of the potlatch tended to be particularistic, and based on kin ties. Thus, the structure of Tlingit society does not indicate that it would become more centralized, solidary, and differentiated under conditions of contact with American or Western societies. Of all the societies encountered thus far, only the Tlingit have norms and values that favor internal competition, extensive social inequality, and material acquisitiveness, all of which have affinities with the cultures of Western societies. Nevertheless, Tlingit institutions must be considered within their own social context; they do not form one-to-one correspondences with Western inequality, materialism, or competitive self-interest.

Formating the Alaska Native Brotherhood (ANB)

The earliest sustained contact that Tlingit had with Westerners came through the fur trade in the eighteenth century. The Russians had colonized Alaska in the late eighteenth century, but had not succeeded in politically subduing the Tlingit. The fur trade, representing a new source of wealth, opened up new opportunities for the Tlingit. By the 1820s, the Tlingit had overexploited their supplies of tradeable furs, and thereafter monopolized trade routes to the interior tribes. Those houses closest to the trade routes had an economic advantage, and consequently rose in wealth and rank.

In 1867 the United States purchased Alaska from Russia, but it did not establish an administrating government until 1877. The Tlingit in Alaska came under less administrative domination than the Indians who were put on reservations in the lower 48. The territorial and civil rights of the Alaska natives had not been defined in the Alaska sale. In 1878 the first fish canneries opened at Klawock and Sitka, and soon several canning companies had appropriated the traditional salmon runs of the Tlingit. In 1897 the native fisherman were prohibited from using fish traps, which had been used for generations for subsistence. The Tlingit had no legal recourse against the intrusions of the fishing companies, and most lost control over their subsistence livelihood. Many Tlingit turned to commercial fishing, and others, mainly women, turned to wage labor in the canning plants (Tollefson 1978:6–10).

Many Tlingit actively participated in the new labor markets and took advantage of commercial fishing opportunities (Krause 1956:115, 231; Drucker 1958:10). House headmen encouraged their kinfolk to accept the new economic opportunities (Klien 1980:996–1,004; Drucker 1965:218–220). Tlingit were not necessarily seeking wealth for economic reinvestment, but to pursue traditional goals of raising personal and house prestige through the potlatch system (Klien 1980; Rogers 1960:179; Wyatt 1984). House leaders did not oppose the exploitation of market opportunities, even though young people began to reject the discipline of the economically communal house. Many moved to towns, started to invest in American-style homes, and became more interested in personal accumulation. By the 1890s the younger generations were less willing to live under the constraints of the house and less willing to share economic wealth. Strong identification with house and clan remained, but house control over individual economic action weakened (Olsen 1967:v, 5; Tollefson 1978:10). Material contributions to and participation in house activities became increasingly voluntary.

Several critical conditions and events arose near the turn of the twentieth century. The Tlingit population was noticeably declining and by 1900 had reached a low point of about 5,000, having declined from an earlier estimated population of 10,000. The potlatch ceremonies were coming under increasing censure from American missionaries, who regarded them as a waste of material resources and a pagan rite that emphasized ancestor worship. Perhaps the last great, traditional potlatch occurred in 1904; by 1912 the potlatches were banned, and some ceremonial goods and artifacts were confiscated by the US government (Metcalfe 1985:7). The economic situation of many Tlingit, too, was declining, and it was becoming more and more difficult to provide the massive displays of wealth required for the potlatch.

As a result, several modifications in the organization of the potlatch were made. The ceremonies became reciprocal between both moieties, rather than between houses related through marriage, and several houses pooled their resources to underwrite the expenses of the potlatch. Thus the ceremony was extended to include members of all clans from both moieties, and now involved the symbolic participation of the entire society and thus promoted more extensive social integration (Tollefson 1977:23-24). Despite the official ban on potlatches, they continued under different guises and in modified form. The more conservative northern villages held more strongly to the potlatch rituals; the southern villages tended to modify their rituals and incorporate them into Russian Orthodox ceremonies or the events of other Christian groups.

As American citizens began to outnumber natives in southeast Alaska, the Tlingit were reduced to minority status. In 1902 the US government established the Tongass National Forest, appropriating nearly 16 million acres of land that had been claimed by the southeastern natives. Territorial dispossession and changing economic conditions and relations were major problems among the Tlingit, but the issue of civil rights was also considered important (Drucker 1965:222).

In 1912 the Alaska Native Brotherhood (ANB) held its first organizational meeting at Juneau in the office of the superintendent of the Bureau of Indian Affairs. In 1915 an auxiliary organization, the Alaska Native Sisterhood (ANS), was formed. Native leaders had observed the organization of the Alaska territorial government and thought that only through a territory-wide native organization could native Alaskans defend and further their interests in civil rights and economic incorporation and protect the subsistence economy. ANB was originally created to facilitate the Alaska native transition to American economic life and citizenship. Its roots — it was organized primarily by Tlingits and one Tsimshian — did not derive primarily from traditional culture and organization, but was organized along the model of a Presbyterian religious society. During the late 1880s up to the early 1900s, Russian Orthodox clergy had organized several religious societies, such as St. Gabriel's Brotherhood and St. Michael's Brotherhood. "These early organizations provided experience in the techniques of group cooperation; officers were elected, business meetings were conducted by rules of parliamentary procedure, funds were raised and campaigns waged for worthy causes. The founders of the Alaska Native Brotherhood had all participated in religious societies. The experience they gained proved fundamental to the establishment of the ANB" (Metcalfe 1985:8). The founder of ANB, Peter Simpson, was greatly influenced by his experience at Sitka Industrial Training School, a Presbyterian school that was started in 1882 and taught native children throughout the southeast. "It is doubtful that the organizers could have done as effective a job or sacrificed so much without the religious commitment and personal dedication they had to their cause" (Hope 1975:2). The original founders were joined by other Tlingit who were educated in the lower 48; together, they set forth a program that encouraged Christian morality, economic entrepreneurship, education, civil government, civil rights, attainment of American citizenship, preservation of native history, and improved health and labor conditions for those working in the canneries (*The Alaska Fisherman* 1980:1; Drucker 1958:3, 32–34).

By the late 1920s ANB had received support and participation from nearly all the villages in the Alaska panhandle. ANB promoted political integration on the basis of Christian principles of individual social responsibility and commitment. It was not organized by traditional social structural principles, but the members embraced Christian principles of voluntary participation and attitudes of progress and change. In fact, the early founders — and some contemporary leaders — refused to recognize traditional culture and kinship organization. ANB's written constitution scrupulously adhered to parliamentary procedures.

Thus, ANB represented a centralization and differentiation of political organization among the Tlingit. The values, organization, and mode of political integration of the new organization were based largely on Christian principles rather than on Tlingit values. The new political center was differentiated from kinship and Tlingit mythology. ANB leaders supported increased social solidarity through participation in potlatches and also promoted a more secular political solidarity through commitments to the organization.

Until the early 1950s ANB formally disassociated itself from traditional culture and social order. In the 1950s potlatches were again openly celebrated, and many Tlingit wished to have dances and ceremonies during recreational periods of ANB grand camp meetings. This led to bitter debate, but ended with the approval of dances and traditional entertainment. Despite the formal differentiation of ANB organization from Tlingit culture and social organization, ANB is informally supported by Tlingit social order. The clan-moiety system and potlatch ceremonies provided an underlying social consensus in support of the organization and its goals. Clan leaders urged participation in ANB, and the traditional generosity of giving wealth away at potlatches was in part transferred to giving material and service contributions to support ANB. Families and individuals gained community recognition for their regular and sizable contributions in support of ANB, just as they had gained recognition in their support of potlatches. The selection of leaders in ANB conformed to Tlingit norms; those who gave service, made contributions, and showed themselves competent advanced to more important positions of leadership and recognition. Again, mobility within ANB closely resembled mobility within the older potlatch social hierarchy. Nevertheless, kinship and clan affiliation did not play a central role in selecting ANB officers. The candidates ran as individuals; they did not appeal to clan loyalties, and it was not uncommon for several men from the same clan to seek election to the same office.

Prior to 1960, ANB attempts to incorporate Aleuts, Eskimos, Athapascans, and other Alaska natives failed. ANB became largely an organization of the natives in the Alaska panhandle — the Tlingit, Haida, and Tsimshian. All three of these groups shared a dual moiety system — Eagle and Raven — and participate in the contemporary, moiety-based potlatch ceremonies.

As a political organization ANB has a long record of distinguished service. It successfully challenged discriminatory laws. For example, in 1922 a chief from Wrangell, Charlie Jones, challenged the Alaska law prohibiting Alaska natives from voting. ANB defended Jones in court and secured the right to vote. In 1924 ANB lobbied in Congress to gain the right of American citizenship for American Indians. Between 1929 and 1959 ANB successfully engineered a land claim suit against the United States for its appropriation of the Tongass and Glacier Bay national parks. In 1929 its lawyers secured the right for native children to attend public schools. In 1945 the Alaska territorial government passed an antidiscrimination law as the result of intense lobbying by ANB leaders. In 1946 several ANB leaders were elected to the Alaska territorial House and Senate. During the 1920s and 1930s the organization represented cannery workers in labor disputes and attempted to gain better wages and better working conditions; its union activities were later turned over to the Congress of Industrial Organization. ANB continues to be active in protecting the subsistence economy for Alaska natives against state, federal, and international laws restricting hunting and fishing rights. In 1968 the southeast natives were awarded $7.5 million for lands lost in the early part of the century, a decision that brought to a close a land claim movement initiated in 1929. ANB is highly mobilized within Alaska state politics; its members are expected to vote and help get voters to the polls. Its strategy has always been one of working within the American political order, never one of challenging that order.

Further Economic and Political Differentiation

Over the past three decades Tlingit economic and political organizations have become more specialized, and the kinship-ceremonial complex continues to provide a consensual ground for further institutional differentiation and change. In 1959, the Tlingit-Haida Central Council (THCC) won the long-standing land claim case. THCC was created by ANB in 1939 to pursue the land claim against the United States; the ANB, which was open to universal membership, could not represent the specific land claims of the Tlingit and Haida tribes. THCC was delegated administration of the $7.5 settlement claim. After some controversy, the Tlingit and Haida decided to keep the settlement money as a capital fund and spend only the interest to provide services to the Tlingit and Haida people. In the lower 48 land claims are usually distributed per capita and therefore do not provide a financial base for government or economic enterprise.

In recent years THCC has come to operate much in the same way as the reservation governments in the lower 48, except that THCC is not subject to direct administrative controls and veto powers from BIA. THCC manages social welfare programs and acts for the legal interests of the Tlingit and Haida of Alaska. Under the legislation of the Self-Determination Act of 1975, THCC has assumed greater administrative responsibility and control over a wide variety of education, economic development, and social welfare programs. THCC lobbies with the Alaska state and federal government and represents the southeast natives in the state-wide organization of the Alaska Federation of Natives (AFN).

THCC is led by a president and six vice-presidents, all of whom comprise the executive committee. The convention meets every two years, and the executive committee is elected to a two-year term. Each community with at least 100 registered Tlingit or Haida voters can send a delegate to the biannual convention. Most villages in southeast Alaska have representatives; other delegates represent communities from Washington, California, and Anchorage (Metcalfe 1985:20). Each community has one delegate and one vote for each 100 registered voters. THCC meetings are conducted according to parliamentary procedures in the same tradition as ANB. The unpaid and voluntary posts in ANB are often considered training grounds for those who wish to aspire to the more administratively responsible and materially rewarding posts in THCC.

Since 1971, the formation of the Sealaska Corporation has introduced a powerful economic institution into southeast Alaska. The Alaska Native Claims Settlement Act of 1971 (ANCSA) authorized the creation of 12 regional economic corporations and numerous village corporations. ANCSA was the result of intense lobbying and grew out of the energy conditions of the late 1960s (more will be said on this in Chapter 7). ANCSA authorized that the regional corporations would control most of the money and land granted by the act — $962.5 million and 44 million acres of land – which was intended to ensure that BIA did not gain direct control over Alaska native land, money, and organizations. The Alaska native leadership, familiar with the administrative controls that BIA exercised over the reservation governments and communities in the lower 48, considered such control a major obstacle to self-government and economic self-sufficiency. Most Alaska natives, however, knew little about corporate economic enterprises. The relative absence of BIA administrative regulation over Alaska native corporations and community associations allowed the Alaska natives considerable political and economic freedoms, freedoms not generally available to the native communities of the lower 48. Nevertheless, freedom from regulation also entails the risk of business losses, and therefore losses of land, money, and other assets. The corporations are profit-oriented organizations, and as such must compete in the domestic and international markets. Possible bankruptcy will mean the loss of native control over land and assets.

About 16,000 native people in southeast Alaska were initially granted 100 shares of stock in Sealaska, which had total assets of $400 million. Shareholders have the right to elect members to the board of directors, which is responsible for Sealaska's economic performance. Since Sealaska controls most Tlingit and Haida natural and economic resources, membership on the board and corporate management jobs have become the most prestigious posts in contemporary Tlingit-Haida society. Sealaska wields considerably more economic power and material and political resources than either THCC or ANB, and hence has attracted much of the experienced and able leadership. Election to the board of directors is a highly competitive and expensive undertaking. Mobilizing kinship ties helps to some extent, but one must also have administrative experience, some business acumen, and proven ability to compete within the American economy.

Overall Sealaska has not shown strong returns on its initial investment. Some corporations have invested their initial settlement money in interest-bearing instruments and have collected higher returns. The Sealaska board of directors, however, has taken an active approach in investing and managing a variety of businesses, and it has argued that this active approach will prove more beneficial in terms of experience, economic autonomy, and generation of jobs than a passive investment approach. During the early 1980s Sealaska's annual revenues were around $250 million, which placed it on the Fortune 1000 list. However, a combination of poor market conditions and a few unfortunate business decisions have contributed to Sealaska's marginal profitability.

Sealaska aggressively invests in and manages a portfolio of companies engaged in construction, sea transportation, lumbering, and fishing. It has also made special efforts to employ qualified shareholders, and about 17 percent of the work force are shareholders. Although it has a firm commitment to profitability and viability within the American corporate world, one of Sealaska's major goals is to preserve the heritage of land and culture. Many members of the community believe that Sealaska must ultimately serve this latter purpose.

Whether Sealaska will achieve its long-range goals of profitability and cultural preservation remains to be seen. In 1991 Sealaska shareholders will have the right to vote for public sale of shares or for keeping the shareholders exclusively among the southeastern natives and their descendents. Up until 1988, the original ANCSA law required that all shares of the regional corporations become available for public sale in 1991. This stipulation greatly agitated the Alaska native community, because it implied that the corporations might well be bought by larger American corporations, thereby leaving the land and natural resources in the hands of American corporate managers. AFN was able to secure a change in the ANCSA law, which now gives the shareholders the right to vote on selling shares publicly. The general opinion appears to be that the shareholders of ANCSA corporations will vote not to make shares available to the general public.

Over the past century the Tlingit and Haida of Alaska have demonstrated a capacity for political and economic institution building. At present, Sealaska, THCC, ANB, and the traditional kinship-ceremonial complex act in concert in their pursuit of Tlingit and Haida political, economic, and cultural interests. The relations of key participants in the four major institutions resemble interlocking corporate directorships. Members of Sealaska's board are often people who have served as past presidents or members on the executive committee of THCC, have put in long service as members of ANB, and often are members of ANB's executive committee. Most people who are active in ANB, THCC, and the Sealaska Corporation also bear the obligations of leadership of their clan in contemporary potlatch ceremonies. Some are heads of their clans, members of the board of directors of Sealaska, and leaders in both THCC and ANB all at the same time, although this is not common. ANB is considered the most respected of the newly differentiated institutions, although in more recent years Sealaska's economic power and, to a much lesser extent, THCC's control over governmental resources, have eclipsed the role of ANB.

Social Change in Southeast Alaska

A combination of conditions are necessary for explaining Tlingit and Haida political and economic institution building. First, the Alaska geopolitical environment, which did not entail BIA administrative regulation over native institutions, contributed to the possibilities for Tlingit-Haida institution building. Similar levels of economic and political differentiation and institutional stability are not generally found among the reservation communities of the lower 48. Second, the competitive, acquisitive, and hierarchical orientations of Tlingit society facilitated active participation in markets and acceptance of American competitive and stratified economic and political institutions. Third, the Tlingit-Haida moiety and potlatch system provided a consensual social solidarity that supported more differentiated political institutions designed to protect native interests within the context of American political institutions and market economy. For example, a combined Eagle and Raven, which symbolizes the societal unity for the Tlingit and Haida as well as Tsimshian, composes the logo for both ANB and the Sealaska Corporation. Fourth, the interpenetration of American and Christian values and organizational models among the leaders of ANB is critical to understanding the formation of the more differentiated and politically integrated ANB, since traditionally particularistic house loyalties were not the basis of ANB's political unity or organization.

The most critical component appears to be the underlying social solidarity of the potlatch system, since without consensus we would expect that the introduction of more differentiated forms of political organization and new norms of political solidarity would fail to become institutionalized and would break the community into conservative and "progressive" factional cleavages, as we have seen among the Sioux on the plains. Prior to 1960, the relative freedom from administrative regulation within the Alaska political environment did not lead to similar developments in political centralization and differentiation and economic incorporation among the Athapascans, Aleuts and Eskimos, who were also resident native groups in Alaska over the same period as the Tlingit and Haida. As Chapter 7 will show, the situation changed drastically after 1960, but the southeastern natives with their moiety structure, potlatch complex, and competitive, hierarchical, and acquisitive cultural orientations were actively engaged in economic entrepreneurship, wage labor, and political institution building well before the political movements of the 1960s in Alaska. Consequently, Tlingit social solidarity and cultural orientations help explain their relative propensity for adopting political and economic change.

Chapter 7

American Indian Social Movements

S o far we have observed change within individual societies, but the emergence of a variety of social movements also illustrates Native American responses to Western contact. Prior to 1900 a considerable number of revitalization movements, some of them transocietal, emerged from a variety of societies. Several of the movements have survived; others lasted only a few years and did not significantly influence institutional order or subsequent historical events.

Among the surviving movements are the peyote cult, or Native American Church; the Handsome Lake Church; the Shaker Church and its variants; the remnants of the Kickapoo prophet's congregation; the Shoshone Sun Dance and its variant among the Crow; and the two Cherokee Keetoowah societies. The peyote cult and the Shaker movement have influenced several groups; the Native American Church currently has more than 200,000 adherents in the plains and southwest and is the most popular of the new native religions. The Big House religion among the Delaware originated in the first Delaware revitalization movement in the early 1760s; it was reformed by the Munsee prophetess in 1805 and lasted until the early 1900s. Although the Delaware religion died out, it was active for about 150 years and therefore must be considered a fully institutionalized movement.

A variety of movements did not survive, among them the Red Stick movement among the Creeks (1813–1814); the Pueblo Revolt in the 1680s and 1690s; the Western Confederacy; Pontiac's Rebellion in the

1760s; the Ghost Dances of 1870 and 1890; the Snake movements among the Creek, Chickasaw, and Choctaw during the 1890s and early 1900s; and the Cherokee movement of 1811–1813. Most of these movements were strongly fundamentalist and opposed to accepting American social, political, economic, and cultural innovations. Some of the overtly militant movements — the Pueblo Revolt, Pontiac's Rebellion — were directly repressed by military force. The Iroquois organized the Western Confederacy during the second half of the seventeenth century as a military threat to strategically play off both the French and British colonies. The loose alliance of Indian nations from the Old Northwest fought in Pontiac's Rebellion, the American Revolution, and the border wars of 1783–1795, and also fought with the British during the War of 1812. Although the strategy of wielding the western Indian nations into a defensive military league had been entertained for nearly a century and a half (1670s to 1817), it never gained a unity or organization that enabled it to become a sustained and effective military or political force. Tribal and subtribal identities and loyalties (Edmunds 1983:92–93, 189), and the primarily subsistence-oriented hunting, gathering, and horticultural economies of these nations, combined with their dependency on manufactured goods, prevented the Indian allies from fielding prolonged military campaigns.

Other movements, such as the Creek, Chickasaw, and Choctaw Snake movements, rallied against the allotment of land and dissolution of their governments, were quelled by troops and police. The Snakes were forced to comply with the new laws that dismantled the governments of the so-called Five Civilized Tribes, and none of these movements survived long into the twentieth century.

The Cherokee movement of 1811–1813 and the Shawnee prophet's movement of 1806–1811 collapsed for internal reasons. Several Cherokee prophets predicted that nonbelievers would be killed in a fiery hailstorm, and when the predictions did not come true the prophets and the movement were abandoned. Similarly the Shawnee prophet, who preached a fundamentalist doctrine against American agriculture and religion, lost his followers after the Battle of Tippecanoe. The prophet had predicted that his powers and rites would protect his congregation from American bullets and weapons. Based on this belief the warriors attacked an American military force sent to constrain the prophet's activities and suffered significant casualties. The survivors refused to follow the prophet's teachings, and he was scorned and humiliated (Edmunds 1983). The Shawnee prophet's movement was over before the beginning of the War of 1812, and his brother Tecumseh led the western allied Indians not in the capacity of war leader of the Shawnee prophet's movement, but as head warrior of the Western Confederacy.

Similarly, the second Ghost Dance movement failed after predictions of the return of the buffalo and ancestors did not come true. The massacre of more than 200 Sioux Ghost Dancers at Wounded Knee in 1890 by American troops, and subsequent American repressive measures against the movement, contributed to its decline. The dancing continued only for a few more years, until it became clear that the prophet Wovoka's predictions would not come to pass (Campbell 1988:232). Only a few tribes and scattered groups continued the rituals, and the Ghost Dance did not become a permanent part of the culture or institutional order of most groups that initially participated in it.

Of the surviving movements, several were influenced by Protestant Christian teachings, although selectively reinterpreted within an Indian world view. The Handsome Lake Church was influenced by Quaker teachings. The Kickapoo prophet, Kenekuk, adapted both Catholic and Protestant teachings (Herring 1988:35). The Native American Church, which emphasized individual responsibility, individual morality, and avoidance of dogmatic doctrine, derives in part from Protestant teachings (Hertzberg 1971:244–245, 248–251). The Christian branch of the Keetoowah Society was composed largely of Baptists and other Protestant Cherokee; the conservative Nighthawk Keetoowah, however, have since the 1890s revived the clan and religious organization of Cherokee society and rejected Christianity. The Christian Keetoowahs actively engage in American institutions by pursuing legal, political, and social welfare issues; the more conservative Nighthawks claim that the Keetoowah Society is a religious institution, not a political organization.

Other groups, such as the Shaker Church and the Shoshone-Crow Sun Dance, have adopted some Christian elements, but largely work within traditional world views of maintaining community and individual health and well-being (Jorgensen 1972:182, 212–221). The early Shaker Church emphasized that because the Creator had given the earth, animals, and plants to humankind, they could not be unnecessarily destroyed or sold. This doctrine legitimated community resistance against farming and the sale of land to the Americans. Smohalla, the Shaker prophet, did not advocate violence against the Americans but his teachings conveyed a divine sanction for the northwestern Indians to resist allotment of land and the reservation system (Trafzer and Beach 1986:73–76).

Most movements were born under conditions of duress, in which a community was threatened by the loss of a subsistence base, political autonomy, or territory; or was experiencing demographic declines or the absence of social and political solidarity; or was finding that the old institutional order inhibited potential avenues of change (Champagne 1983c, 1985, 1988). However, not all Indian nations responded with or adopted revitalization movements.

Many religious revitalization movements were initiated by an ethical and law-giving prophet (Lewis 1988:221–227; Champagne 1988) who was given instructions by the Creator for a plan to revive a whole culture or society. The Sweet Medicine myth of the Cheyenne, the events of which are believed to have occurred as late as 1775, is a good archetypal example. Here the prophet, Sweet Medicine, descended from a sacred mountain and gave the divine law and political organization to the Cheyenne, all of which were designed to accommodate their transition to a new life on the plains. If the Cheyenne obeyed the law and performed the ceremonies, then the Creator would protect and ensure the cultural survival of their nation (Erdoes and Ortiz 1984:199–205). This myth resembles the story of Moses, which had probably been transmitted to them, directly or indirectly, sometime during the colonial period. Some prophets brought commandments of moral reorganization (the Kickapoo prophet and Handsome Lake); others brought messages of militant fundamentalism (the Shawnee prophet and one of the Delaware prophets during the 1760s). Some messages advocated limited acceptance of American agriculture and moral order; others advocated a return to traditional social order and retention of land. Although the content of the messages varied, the goals and methods were always designed to ensure the survival of an Indian nation or nations during a period of extreme duress.

Social Movements in the Twentieth Century

The religious revitalization movements belong to the period prior to 1900. Several movements — most notably the Native American Church, or peyote cult, which was incorporated in 1918 — have thrived in the twentieth century, but most movements that originated in this century have been secular political and social movements, not ones initiated by prophets. One of the earliest of these movements was the Society of American Indians (SAI), founded in 1911. It was modeled after the numerous religious and social societies, such as the YMCA, that were in vogue during the early part of this century; the Alaska Native Brotherhood, founded by the Tlingit in 1912, was in some respects also a manifestation of this same type of movement. SAI was formed by a group of Indian professionals whose goals and orientations reflected the times in which they lived. The organization, like the early ANB, worked toward educating, integrating, and assimilating Indians into American society (Cornell 1988:188, 191; Hertzberg 1971). Torn by internal difficulties, by the 1930s SAI had spent itself. The Indian Defense League, formed in 1926, was primarily concerned with preserving treaty rights and returning territories to the Iroquois of upstate New York.

The 1930s brought the Indian Reorganization Act, in which many tribes were involved. Of the 252 tribes that voted on whether to adopt the IRA, 174 tribes accepted, but only 92 voted to accept an IRA constitutional government and only 71 adopted economic development corporations under its provisions (Kelly 1986:250–251). In 1944, the National Congress for American Indians (NCAI) was formed, largely by Indian members of the Bureau of Indian Affairs. NCAI, designed to protect Indian interests in Washington, has worked largely as a lobbying group. It did not immediately gain widespread support until the 1950s, when it became a focal point for organizing Indian opposition to the termination policy, which was designed to abolish the reservation system and assimilate the Indian population into the American mainstream. Most Indian groups considered the policy a breach of the treaty rights and obligations that preserved the reservations as semisovereign communities. Although more than 100 reservations were terminated, NCAI led an effective opposition, and by 1960 the termination policy was no longer being implemented. In recent years many of the terminated tribes have sued to have their treaty rights and reservations reestablished, most notably the Menominee in Wisconsin during the 1970s.

The termination policies led to the formation of a variety of supratribal organizations during the 1950s and 1960s. Numerous protest movements had sprung up during the 1950s, and in 1961 a major conference took place in Chicago on American Indian policy and issues. Shortly thereafter the National Indian Youth Council (NIYC) was founded, and by 1963 organized protests were rallying against BIA administration. The protest movements reached a high of about 80 during 1971, and then fell to about 50 per year by 1975 (Cornell 1988:188). Although many of the protests focused on local issues, the takeover of Alcatraz Island, the occupation of Wounded Knee in South Dakota, and the pillaging of the BIA central offices in Washington gained prolonged national attention. One of the major urban militant groups was the American Indian Movement (AIM), founded in Minneapolis in 1968. It was initially formed to provide urban Indian community members with self-defense against police harassment, but by 1970 AIM was involved in a variety of issues and attempted to organize a national movement. AIM members were prominent in the Alcatraz, Wounded Knee, and BIA headquarters incidents (Cornell 1988: 189–190).

The initial response of the more conservative reservation Indians was to disengage themselves from the activities of AIM. Many did not agree with the methods or aims employed by the militant urban organizations, which took the Black Panthers among others as their model. Since the mid-1970s, many AIM leaders have become disillusioned with the possibilities of securing treaty rights within the American system. They have allied with conservative reservation Indians, and with world indigenous peoples' organizations and in order to seek international recognition of their treaty and national rights in the United Nations. The result, the International Indian Treaty Council (IITC), founded in 1974, has held several international conferences in Geneva under the auspices of UNESCO and has gained nongovernmental organization (NGO) status at the UN. IITC and allied indigenous nations around the world have presented their positions at several international conferences; the UN, however, while sympathetic and generally supportive, will not take the step to recognize the indigenous nations as independent nationalities (Josephy 1984:254–255).

The Alaska Native Claims Settlement Act

The 1960s and 1970s saw the birth of several relatively successful Indian rights movements. Several terminated tribes regained federal recognition, two Maine tribes regained over $80 million and rights to buy land, the Taos pueblo regained sacred land, and the tribes of the northwest and Wisconsin have engaged in continuous struggle and negotiation with state governments over fishing rights.

Perhaps the most innovative land claim settlement was the Alaska Native Claims Settlement Act (ANCSA) of 1971. This settlement granted $962.5 million and 44 million acres of land to the Alaska natives. ANCSA has become a model for land claim settlements around the world. Two major land claims settlements in Canada—James Bay and northern Quebec— benefited from the experience of the ANCSA agreement, and Australian aboriginal peoples have studied and observed the act as a possible model for settling land claims in Australia now that that country's government has been increasingly compelled to recognize the claims of the original Australians (ANRC 1984(5):51–53). The long-term results of ANCSA's large-scale social experiment are as yet undetermined.

In comparison to BIA's administration of reservations in the lower 48, the Alaska political environment is much more pluralistic. Most of Alaska's native peoples do not live on reservations and do not live under direct administrative regulation from BIA, state, or federal authorities. There were some IRA village governments and a few reservations, but most came under the laws of the Alaska territorial government; before statehood in 1959, Alaska native civil and land rights were left relatively undefined. Because most villages were located in the interior or in remote areas, there was little need or possibility for consistent state or federal regulation. Villagers fished and hunted for subsistence, and were relatively self-sufficient. Most indigenous groups in Alaska lived in small, independent villages, often with only an informal government of elders. The Tlingit, Haida, and Tsimshian were an exception: although they lived in villages, clan and moiety relations were also a central form of social organization. Alaska native peoples do not form a homogeneous culture or ethnic group, and there has been little ethnogenesis even into the 1980s. The several native Alaskan cultural groups maintain considerable autonomy: Inupiat and Yupik Eskimos, Aleuts, Athapascans, and southeastern Indians (McBeath and Morehouse 1980:13).

Thus the movement that led to ANCSA did not emerge from a social or cultural consensus of Alaska native groups, nor did such a consensus appear during subsequent events. Rather, the movement was one of group solidarity created by events that threatened the interests of Alaska's indigenous groups in preserving land, culture, and a subsistence economy.

The major threat to Alaska's native peoples came from the state of Alaska in the early 1960s. From 1867 to 1959 the land and civil rights of Alaska's indigenous inhabitants were left largely undefined, and except in the southeast little effort was made by Indians or Americans to clarify those relations. These conditions changed in the early 1960s, however. The Athapascan Tanana chiefs grew concerned about the proposed Rampart Dam, which threatened to flood some of their land and significantly disturb the subsistence economy (ANRC 1984(6): 125-130). The Eskimos at Point Hope protested against proposed atomic tests, which would obviously inalterably affect their lives and contaminate caribou herds. Other issues involved state and international bans on the hunting of traditional subsistence foods and increasing regulation of the subsistence economy by state officials. The major common threat, however, came with Alaska's statehood (ANRC 1984(6):160).

In its charter, the state of Alaska was granted administration over 103 million acres of land, much of it already claimed by native communities (Arnold 1978:94-101; ANRC 1984(3):255-256). Upon statehood in 1959, Alaska's efforts to acquire its share of the 375 million acres of Alaska land threatened the interests of the native communities and gave them a basis for political unification. In order to stop the state from selecting land that they wished to reserve, the native communities filed claims to more land than existed in the state. Although many villagers did not have a concept of Western land ownership, events were pressing them to take action (ANRC 1984(6):6-7).

During the early 1960s many Alaska villages joined ANB in hopes that it would protect their interests. Although ANB expanded to more than 100 "camps," its laws prohibited anyone who was not from the southeast from running for chairman, a restriction that alienated many of the members from other regions.

In October 1966 the Alaska Federation of Natives (AFN) was formed in Anchorage. Many of the members who attended did so at the expense of President Johnson's Great Society programs. Since the expense of traveling in Alaska was prohibitive, and because the native administrators of various Office of Economic Opportunity (OEO) programs planned to meet in Anchorage, too, the latter planned their meetings to coincide with the AFN annual convention. The OEO community action programs provided resources to native communities so that they could bring rural leaders together to discuss land claims issues. The OEO programs had just started in the state, and the governor appointed a young Tlingit to administer the programs state-wide. Twelve regional associations composed of loose coalitions of villages formed during this period. AFN was also supported by loans from the Yakima tribe in Washington, loans from villages such as Tyonek, and donations from church groups and other groups. Many well-educated, professional, politically active native Alaskans were attracted to AFN leadership, which was sophisticated, dedicated, and willing to make considerable personal and financial sacrifices (ANRC 1984(4):5–6). The first success for AFN came in 1966 when secretary of the interior Stewart Udall imposed a freeze on all transfers of federal land to the state of Alaska, which allowed time for the settlement of native claims.

In 1968 the Alaska Land Claims Task Force created by Governor Walter Hickle recommended that Alaska's native peoples be granted 40 million acres. This figure was used in subsequent negotiations and bills before the US Congress, but there was as yet little action for settling the claim in Washington. In the same year oil was discovered in Prudhoe Bay, and a consortium of oil and construction companies under the name of Alyeska planned to build a pipeline from Prudhoe Bay to Valdez. These efforts were opposed by native communities, which claimed the land along the planned pipeline route as theirs. The Indians secured a court injunction against pipeline construction until their land claims were settled. In the meantime, Alyeska had already stockpiled millions of dollars worth of construction equipment, which was now depreciating in the harsh Alaska environment (ANRC 1984(6):130). The company's appeals in court failed, and the issue was decided in Congress.

In the negotiations AFN was assisted pro bono by two prominent lawyers, Ramsay Clark and former Supreme Court Justice Arthur Goldberg. The oil companies did not directly participate in the ANCSA negotiations, but their lobbyists pressed congresspeople and the Nixon Administration to move the settlement bill out of committee to secure speedy passage. Alyeska's lobbyists also pressed the government to make concessions to the native inhabitants in order to secure right of way for the pipeline (ANRC 1984(6):130, 1984(3):87; Berry 1975). An unusual coalition of interests – oil companies, the State of Alaska, the Nixon Administration, and the Alaska native communities – negotiated the bill that passed as ANCSA in November 1971.

ANCSA preserved native control over 44 million acres of land, and provided the Alaska native communities with $962.5 million in compensation for surrendering rights to 331 million acres of Alaska territory. In order to avoid BIA administration of the land and control over the funds, 13 regional corporations were formed by the act. Twelve of these were analogous to the 12 regional associations that composed AFN; the 13th corporation was created for Alaska native peoples who did not live in Alaska. The corporations were to distribute the funds according to population. This provision led to a temporary withdrawal of the North Slope region from AFN, because oil had been discovered off the North Slope and the North Slope Association was not given rights to revenues from the oil and could not choose known oil-bearing lands. Consequently the Eskimos of the North Slope were left with little compensation, and had to share the funds of the settlement with more populous regions that had no claim to oil lands.

A complicated formula dictating that all the regions were to share in the profits derived from the sale of minerals led to considerable controversy and expenditure of revenues for clarifying the issues; as of this writing, it has not been satisfactorily resolved. The 13 regional corporations were granted 55 percent of the total settlement, and the remainder was divided among village corporations. The regional corporations were granted control of the settlement lands; the village corporations were allowed to select land, to which they had surface rights; and the subsurface rights remained in the hands of the regional corporation.

The creation of the corporations was a major experiment. The corporations were to manage the money and resources of the act and also enter into competitive market relations. For most Alaska native peoples, the corporate structure was imposed by congressional legislators. Most of the AFN leadership did not have corporate business experience, and so learning to manage the corporations had to be done on the job (Berger 1985:30). ANCSA exempted the corporations from income tax for 20 years, but at the end of that period, in 1991, the corporation's profits would be subject to taxation and their shares would be opened to public sale. This latter condition has created considerable consternation among Alaska's native communities, since it carries a strong possibility that the corporations might be taken over by non-natives, which would imply the loss of land, native culture, and the subsistence economy. AFN lobbied Congress and the Alaska congressional delegation in order to change many of ANCSA's provisions, and in 1988 secured passage of an amendment that allows native shareholders to vote on whether they wish to allow the sale of shares on the open market after 1991. The consensus is that there will not be any public sale of regional corporate stock after 1991.

ANCSA was perhaps one of the most favorable settlements in American history, but many caveats remain. The profit-oriented corporations run the risk of bankruptcy and with it loss of control over the land granted in the settlement. In many cases the orientations of the large-scale, profit-oriented corporations with known assets of several hundred million dollars conflicts with the subsistence-economy lifestyles and orientations of most rural villagers. Although initially all members of a region received 100 shares, many villagers would like to see more concrete economic benefits from the investments and activities of the corporations. Few of the corporations have been economically healthy enough to pay substantial dividends. Furthermore, some village leaders believe that sovereign tribal government powers should have more control over land (Berger 1985:129-131, 138-151). The corporate-village rift has gained momentum during the mid-1980s, and AFN's solution to this issue has been to add the villages as a third layer of organization within the preexisting AFN structure of corporations and regional associations. Nevertheless, the villages have received fewer collective votes than either the regional associations or the corporations. The corporations, which receive the most votes at the annual AFN convention, tend to have the most power within the organization.

The regional corporations have given Alaska's native communities enhanced economic and political power within the Alaska government and economy. AFN has been a highly mobilized political force in Alaska, concerned with a variety of education, subsistence, social welfare, and political issues. The Eskimos of the North Slope have organized the North Slope Borough and now tax the oil companies and workers on Prudhoe Bay (McBeath and Morehouse 1980). Although Alaska's native population is about 17 percent of the total, it comprises 25 percent of the electorate, indicating a greater level of political mobilization than among the general population.

Nevertheless, Alaska's indigenous groups continue to confront massive change, much of it due to ANCSA. The distribution of land has yet to be completed, and many villages have found that under the act they are not able to continue their subsistence lifestyles. The amount of land available to them is now less, and state restrictions and regulations inhibit the exploitation of the open wilderness for hunting. With the deteriorating subsistence economy came a series of economic and social problems — increased dependence on social welfare programs, drug abuse, drinking, and violence.

In the end success of ANCSA will depend on the ability of the regional corporations to survive and prosper. If they do not, then the native communities will lose their remaining land and, with it, much of their heritage. ANCSA was intended to give them control over their own resources and institutions, but the risks involve possible loss of control over the land, a risk considered much too high by many.

The rise of the movement to secure ANCSA was due to combination of conditions: the relatively autonomous Alaska native villages, the availability of resources through the antipoverty programs, a common land and economic threat, a group of sophisticated leaders, the organization of AFN, and the political leverage created by the ability to prevent construction of the Alaska pipeline. Some of these conditions were dependent on the US government: the willingness of a cabinet-level official to freeze Alaska land claims and the willingness of the federal court system to enforce injunctions against pipeline construction. Without this cooperation by the US government, Alaska's native peoples could hardly have defended their interests against the powerful forces arrayed against them. Without leverage over construction of the pipeline and the subsequent indirect support of the oil and construction companies, it is doubtful that Alaska's indigenous groups could have won a settlement as quickly and favorable as ANCSA. AFN has become the major political center for Alaska's native peoples, and its institutionalization has been created in part by a competitive political environment that continually threatens land rights, subsistence economy, and native political interests. AFN has sought to work as an interest group within the US institutional order, and uses its influence over the well-mobilized native voters to command the attention and alliance of the leading state officials and the Alaska congressional delegation.

Chapter 8

Conditions and Strategies for Change

C HAPTERS 2 THROUGH 6 were organized according to region, and noted the considerable variation in institutional order and responses to Western impacts that occurred even within the same ecological zone. This last chapter views the material in yet another way. The case societies of the preceding chapters were categorized into three groups: (1) societies that were socially and politically decentralized with a nondifferentiated political order, (2) societies that had mythically ordained social and/or political orders, and (3) societies that were – or became – socially and politically well integrated with a differentiated polity. Further refinements can be made in each category, and those will be noted when the individual cases are discussed. Given the three classifications, our task will be to discuss the types of change and the conditions under which change occurred.

Decentralized and Nondifferentiated Societies

This first group is composed of the Crow, the Quechan, the Sioux, the Navajo, the Delaware prior to 1760, the Choctaw prior to 1860, and the Tlingit prior to 1912. During the time periods under discussion each of these societies did not have a centralized political order and its social and political identifications were local and/or tied to kinship groups. Hence, there were limited grounds for sustained social or political cohesion.

The Delaware prior to 1760 were organized into decentralized, kin-based bands. Although pre-1760 the Delaware were increasingly marginalized politically and economically, they were not subject to the strict reservation administrations that the Crow, Sioux, and others were. In the early 1760s the conditions of relative freedom from direct administration and of major political, military, and economic threats from the British contributed to the Delaware formation of a national revitalization movement that integrated the three major Delaware bands religiously, socially, militarily, and politically. The Delaware, through the religious approval of their lawgiving prophets, formed a more centralized social and political order. The prophets introduced notions — most likely gathered and reinterpreted from Christian sources — of divine retribution, and they introduced a greater sense of tension between the sacred and profane realms designed to mobilize the Delaware to accept change despite their decentralized social order and traditionalistic world view. The Delaware societal order, however, remained nondifferentiated among polity, kinship, and religion. Thus the Delaware responded to the pressures of the early 1760s with increased social and cultural integration, but not with increased societal differentiation.

Both the Quechan and Sioux gave political identification to local kinship groups. Although the Quechan and several major Sioux reservations accepted IRA governments in the 1930s, they experienced considerable difficulties in participating in and normatively institutionalizing the new, centralized, more representative governments. Several Sioux reservations, especially, have long-standing conflicts between allegiances to the IRA governments and to the local kin-based leaders, and also have little consensus over the fundamental rules of political order. Both the Quechan and Sioux have been strongly fundamentalist and resistant to change, but they have strong commitments to group survival and political autonomy.

The Navajo had a decentralized political structure in which local headmen led kin-based bands. However, US officials and interests in extraction of Navajo natural resources led to American-inspired efforts to form a central government, a government that did not gain the support of most local headmen. The opportunity presented in 1937 by a Navajo convention to write a constitution was lost when US officials deemed that the new constitution would allow the Navajo too much freedom from bureaucratic regulation. Thus the Navajo were saddled with the Rules of 1938, which more or less dictated the form of the Navajo tribal council. Local chapters, which were led by traditional leaders, were incorporated into the tribal government structure in 1955 in an attempt to generate broader political participation. In 1959 and thereafter the Navajo created an independent judiciary, designed to keep local states from usurping administration of law and order on the Navajo reservation. The judicial system has become an increasingly important semiautonomous organization within the tribal government.

During recent years the Navajo government has become increasingly bureaucratized because of antipoverty programs and extensive mining and export of raw materials. Nevertheless, the rise of a more centralized and differentiated Navajo tribal government was instigated largely by US officials and American mining interests; it cannot be seen as a development arising from the norms and values of the decentralized Navajo communities. Incorporating chapters into the government helped bring the local leaders and communities into a unified Navajo political order, but the norms, world view, and political organization of the chapters continue to operate along Navajo political traditions, not along the centralized and instrumentally rationalized world views that many Navajo leaders and US officials feel are necessary to manage a large, bureaucratic government and the business of a major domestic supplier of raw materials.

The Crow, organized by local bands and clans, rejected the IRA government and adopted their own constitution in 1960. This constitution, however, did not differentiate polity from society, but rather allowed the entire adult population to form the tribal council. Given the rules of the Crow constitution, the political order allows the free play of traditional Crow political rules, which emphasize kinship ties and charismatic, religiously legitimated leadership. The Crow constitution does not challenge traditional political values and norms, and consequently the rules of the political order are not openly challenged, as among the Sioux and Navajo, or often disregarded, as among the Quechan.

The Choctaw, who were organized into three political districts and local kinship groups, each with its own leader, formed a centralized constitutional government in 1860. Several conditions favored Choctaw political centralization and differentiation. First, the Choctaw were not subject during this period to the direct reservation administration. Second, they retained their subsistence base and were incorporated into agricultural markets. Third, they formed a class structure with entrepreneurial planters, and the planters and American-educated Choctaw strongly favored adopting a constitutional government.

Nevertheless the Choctaw had difficulties forming a centralized constitutional government, despite encountering conditions similar to those encountered by the Cherokee, who formed their constitutional government between 1809 and 1827. Choctaw regional groups prevented the formation of a centralized government in 1830 and again in 1834. US officials insisted on a Choctaw constitutional government in 1834, but the Choctaw refused to allow their three districts to be centralized under one chief executive.

Between 1834 and 1856, the Choctaw incrementally accepted a more bureaucratic government and the separation of government from kinship. Forging a centralized government, however, required the use of force by the Choctaw planters, who were supported and aided by the US government. The constitution of 1860 was a compromise: it retained the district chiefs as symbols of social and political integration and as a means to help legitimate the newly centralized constitutional government. Thus, as in some of the reservation cases, Choctaw political centralization required American sponsorship and force in face of opposition from conservatives.

The Tlingit prior to 1912 were decentralized politically, with political leadership based on local, kin-based house headmen. Several favorable conditions allowed the Tlingit to move from the decentralized and kin-based political order to a centralized and differentiated polity: the pluralistic and nonreservation Alaska political environment; access to wage labor and commercial fishing markets; continuity of the subsistence economy; the competitive, hierarchical, and acquisitive Tlingit normative order; American threats to civil rights, subsistence, and land; the Tlingit acceptance of Christian religion, values, and forms of organization; and the further integration of the potlatch and moiety complex. These conditions laid the social and political foundations for the Alaska Native Brotherhood, which in turn led to the Tlingit-Haida Central Council and to the founding of Sealaska Corporation. In contrast to political change on many reservations and among the Choctaw, the formation of the more differentiated Tlingit political institutions was predominantly consensual.

Decentralized and kin-based societies experienced several conditions that favored consensual change: retention of subsistence economy, incorporation into new markets, relative freedom from direct administrative regulation, strong external threats to political and economic autonomy, and reinterpretation and extension of the institutions of social and political solidarity. Of the reservation societies, the Navajo made the most far-reaching institutional changes. They, unlike the Crow, Sioux, and Quechan, retained their subsistence economy, which aided the organization of the chapters and the political activism in the communities. Through a revitalization movement the Delaware adopted religiously integrated social and political institutions; the movement, however, did not lead to greater political differentiation. The Delaware prophets made their changes (1760s) before the model of the differentiated American polity was available, and in many respects the Delaware centralization resembles the religious integration of the nondifferentiated Iroquois Confederacy. In fact, the Delaware were very familiar with Iroquois political institutions. The Tlingit took their political model from Christian societies and organized ANB as a response to threatening political and economic conditions. But as the Choctaw case shows, favorable conditions (relative freedom from administrative regulation, retention of subsistence economy, market incorporation, external threats to land and political autonomy, and groups or classes advocating adoption of differentiated political institutions) are not sufficient for a consensual institutionalization of a differentiated, constitutional government. Prior to 1860 most Choctaw refused to accept this form of government, preferring to uphold the autonomy of their district governments. By comparison, the social integration of Tlingit society through the more extensively defined potlatch moiety system in the early 1900s was critical to creating the social consensus necessary for the institutionalization of ANB. The absence of such institutions among the Navajo, Quechan, and Sioux suggests that it is doubtful that their relatively differentiated reservation governments are fully institutionalized by conservative members of their societies.

Societies with Mythically Defined National, Social, and/or Political Orders

These societies can be divided into two subgroups, depending on whether collective political or social commitments take precedence over loyalties to local or kinship groups. The Iroquois, the Delaware from 1760 on, and the Creek all had decentralized social and political organization; the Northern Cheyenne, the Arapahoe, and the Chickasaw, however, all had more centralized social and political loyalties. We would expect different forms of response from these two groups; all things being equal, the more decentralized societies should find it more difficult to mount sustained, collective movements and institutionalize a more differentiated political order.

The Iroquois, Delaware, and Creek showed strong, fundamentalist resistance to economic and political change and little capacity for consensual institutional change or increased political solidarity. The members of the mythically ordained Iroquois Confederacy gave their political loyalties primarily to kinship groups and clans. The Iroquois showed relatively little political solidarity during the 1700s, and major changes came through the Handsome Lake Church, which reordered Iroquois culture and legitimated changes in family organization, moral order, and male farming roles that eased the Iroquois transition to reservation life in the early 1800s. During the 1800s the Iroquois became increasingly fragmented politically, with groups leaving for Canada, Oklahoma, and Wisconsin and many reservation communities divided into Christian and traditional factions. Conservative Iroquois still cling to the confederacy and to Iroquois culture, and during this century they have worked to regain land and treaty rights. Although many Iroquois have retained their traditional world views and social organization, they have not formed stronger political loyalties, and as a society or confederacy they have not adopted more centralized or differentiated political institutions.

The Delaware formed a religiously integrated social and political order in the 1760s, but the three political divisions were also kin-based phratries that commanded the primary social and political loyalties. Between 1760 and 1867, most Delaware resisted the influences of American farming, religion, and political organization. A fundamentalist movement in 1805 formalized the rituals of the Big House religion and taught a return to the traditional lifestyle and a rejection of American innovations. The events sparked by the Shawnee prophet in 1806 resulted in the formation of a central chief and an assistant over the three political phratries, a form of government that lasted until 1867 when the main body of Delaware joined the Cherokee nation, then in Oklahoma. An attempt to form a constitutional government in the early 1860s failed because most Delaware simply ignored it. Thus the Delaware were strongly fundamentalist and resisted change in political and economic organization.

The Creek social and political order was organized into red and white towns and red and white clans within the towns. The red-white symbolism reflected Creek views of the dualist forces in the universe. Much of Creek history can be interpreted as a struggle between leading white towns and leading red towns. Political and social loyalties went primarily to villages and their clan segments; villages claimed religious and political autonomy because of covenants that each ceremonial square upheld with the Great Spirit. During the nineteenth century, the Creek showed strong, fundamentalist resistance to change despite being in the southeast, where they had a subsistence economy, access to the southern export economy, and a small class of merchants and planters. Despite conscious efforts by US officials and conditions under which the Cherokee formed a differentiated constitutional government in 1827, the Creek resisted adopting more differentiated institutions until 1867. Between 1867 and 1873 the new Creek government was unstable, a majority of Creek being dissatisfied with the new government, which remained in power largely through the recognition and support of the US government.

After 1876 the conservative opposition amounted to about one-third of the population. The conservatives set up their own alternative government, which was not recognized by the Americans. After their defeat in the Green Peach War, the conservative opposition subsided until the mid-1890s, when issues of allotment and national political dissolution aroused conservative ire. Of all the southeastern cases, the Creek case was the last to accept a constitutional system and had the most unstable government.

The Northern Cheyenne and Arapahoe provide examples of social orders in which the religious symbolism is more collective. Both groups were located in the plains and therefore were subject to loss of subsistence economy and regulation on reservations by BIA — both unfavorable conditions for collective action and consensual change. The Northern Cheyenne Sweet Medicine myth provided a set of laws and the political organization for the Council of 44 Chiefs. The covenant required the Cheyenne to honor sacred laws, perform ceremonies, and protect the sacred bundles; in return, the Creator would give his protection. The Northern Cheyenne have strongly resisted change to their culture and political order. The chief and warrior societies were excluded by BIA officials from the early business council and, after the mid-1930s, the IRA government. Until recent decades, these secular governments were largely dominated by the Cheyenne cattle ranchers. The chief and warrior societies, however, continue to operate in organizing ceremonies. The Cheyenne religion creates collective commitments to cultural survival that ideally supersede loyalties to kinship groups and bands. The community rejection of coal strip mining during the 1970s is one example of Northern Cheyenne collective mobilization for cultural survival.

The Arapahoe show a similar pattern of fundamentalism and collective religious commitments to community preservation and moral order. The Arapahoe men were organized into seven mythically integrated age-grades, represented by seven medicine lodges, and these commitments superseded kinship ties. The men of the sixth lodge were the political leaders, and were selected by the elders of the seventh, and highest, lodge. The Arapahoe age-grades did not ordain any particular political structure, as, for instance, did the Council of 44 Chiefs among the Northern Cheyenne, and political roles were differentiated from religious roles, although the highest religious age-grade regulated the political leaders of the sixth age-grade.

This culturally integrated age-grade structure proved resilient to the hardships of the reservation period, and although specific ceremonial knowledge has been lost, the age-grades continue to provide a basis for a relatively solidary and well-integrated Northern Arapahoe community and a stable representative government in the form of a business council. Although the Arapahoe elders rejected the IRA form of government as too threatening to their social-religious order, they incorporated the business council into the age-grade hierarchy. Arapahoe elders are willing to accept change as long as it does not threaten the continuity of their institutional order. In comparison, the Gros Ventre of the plains, a group related to the Arapahoe also organized by age-grades, lost its ceremonial leadership by 1910. Fowler reports that the Gros Ventre at Fort Belknap did not enjoy the same degree of community solidarity and political-moral order as the Northern Arapahoe, implying that the ceremonial integration of the

Arapahoe age-grades is a major condition for community solidarity and political stability.

The Chickasaw prior to 1845 had a ceremonially integrated kinship system in which the national war, civil, and priestly leaders were selected according to kinship group. At Chickasaw ceremonies, the kinship groups arranged themselves according to phratry and rank. This institutional configuration proved capable of binding the Chickasaw together during the period of incessant war between 1730 and 1760. They showed great reluctance to change their nondifferentiated social-religious-political order, even after 1800, despite the formation of a merchant-planter class, contact with missionaries, American threats of removal and threats to the land, the decline of the fur trade, and the transition to subsistence farming and livestock.

The major change in the Chickasaw polity came in the mid-1840s, when the Chickasaw merchant-planters, with the support of the United States, refused to recognize the old government. In the late 1840s the conservatives abandoned the kin-based government and joined the planters in a effort to secure national separation from the Choctaw. This movement created a sense of national political solidarity that, with American intervention, resulted in the formation of a differentiated constitutional government in 1856. Thus there was no consensual transition from the old, nondifferentiated government to the new, constitutional government. Coercion was used to abolish the old government, but the new, differentiated, constitutional government was formed on the basis of a secular political solidarity that formed among the conservatives in their effort to regain national independence.

Socially and Politically Solidary Societies with Differentiated Polities

None of the societies under consideration here had political nationalities and differentiated polities prior to Western contact, and it seems doubtful that they would have taken such a path of political change were it not for this contact. For specific historical periods, several societies can be classified within this group: the Cherokee between 1809 and 1907, the Chickasaw between 1856 and 1907, the Choctaw between 1860 and 1907, and the Tlingit after 1912. The Creek could possibly be added to this list, but their constitutional government was tenuously institutionalized between 1867 and 1884, and by the mid-1890s the conservatives were again challenging the constitutional government, giving the Creek government only a very brief period of stability. The Northern Arapahoe could also be considered, but their government, consisting of an elected business council, is not comparable to the levels of political differentiation obtained by the cases selected here.

By 1800 the Cherokee were exhibiting a mythically integrated, national clan system that was differentiated from political organization. The Cherokee polity had also become increasingly secular, excluding priests from political decision making and influence. The formation of a unified political nationality occurred under removal pressures in 1809. Between 1809 and 1827, under constant pressures from the Americans for surrender of land and removal, the Cherokee increasingly differentiated and centralized their polity, resulting in the constitution of 1827. The Cherokee retained this government until 1907, when the US government abolished the Indian governments in Indian Territory. Several favorable conditions facilitated Cherokee political institution building: American threats to land and political autonomy; transition to a subsistence agricultural economy; incorporation into the southern plantation export economy; the formation of a small group of economic entrepreneurs, planters, and mission-educated Cherokee, who advocated adoption of American political and economic models; the ceremonially integrated, national clan system; and the differentiation of the polity from kinship and religious roles and influence.

Over the same period (1800–1830), the Choctaw, Chickasaw, and the Creek were exposed to similar conditions in the southeast, but they did not follow the path of the Cherokee. Thus the institutional order of Cherokee society was a central cause in the Cherokee response to removal pressures. The Chickasaw were ceremonially integrated at a national level, but their polity was not differentiated from kinship and religious organization, and prior to 1830 they were strongly opposed to change in their institutional order. The Choctaw were decentralized and their polity was embedded in local kinship groups, which contributed to their failure to institutionalize a centralized government in 1830. The Creek were decentralized socially and politically and their polity was symbolically ordered, and they showed strong resistance to political and economic change prior to 1836.

The other southeastern nations adopted constitutional governments 30–40 years later than the Cherokee, after they were removed to Indian Territory. The Chickasaw formed their constitutional government only after the old, nondifferentiated government was abolished by the planters and the US government and after the conservatives had abandoned the old political form in favor of a unified separatist movement from the Choctaw nation in the 1840s and early 1850s. The Choctaw formed a constitutional government in 1834 under American pressure, but did not centralize the government until 1860, when they were forced to do so by the Choctaw planters and their American supporters. The new government was legitimated by the district chiefs, who thereafter functioned primarily as symbols of social and political integration. The Creek, with their decentralized and nondifferentiated societal order, strongly resisted change and were last among the major southeastern societies to adopt a constitutional government. They experienced the greatest instability over institutionalizing the differentiated constitutional form of government. The less solidary and differentiated southeastern societies formed their differentiated constitutional governments later than the Cherokee, and they used more coercion and, in the Creek case, experienced considerable normative instability.

The Tlingit followed a path to consensual political integration and differentiation comparable to that of the Cherokee. The conditions in the early 1900s are roughly comparable to those in the southeast between 1800 and 1830. The Tlingit were subject to American threats to territory but not to reservation administration; they retained their subsistence fishing economy and were incorporated into commercial fishing and wage labor markets; and a small group of Christianized leaders emerged to vigorously advocate American citizenship and economic, social, and political lifestyle while the Tlingit were extending the integrative aspects of the potlatch to encompass both moieties, or, in other words, the entire society.

As we have seen from comparing the southeastern cases, all these factors are necessary but not sufficient conditions to explain the rise of the differentiated Cherokee government. Hence, these conditions cannot be sufficient causes of Tlingit political institution building. The Cherokee and Tlingit share a ceremonially integrated kinship system, which in the Cherokee case was differentiated from political organization. The differentiation of polity and kinship came for the Tlingit with the introduction of ANB, which gained widespread support from clan leaders, who did not insist that it recognize clan prerogatives. The social support from the influential clan elders and their acceptance of a differentiated polity, then, laid the foundation for the consensual institutionalization of the centralized and differentiated organization of ANB.

It is probably worth noting that the differentiated constitutional governments emerged in the southeast and in Alaska during periods when there was an absence of direct administrative regulation from the US government. By 1907 the governments of the four major southeastern societies were abolished. In recent decades, however, they have regained the right to limited self-government under rules and regulations that closely resemble reservation settings. Nevertheless, freedom from direct administrative regulation is not sufficient to account for the institutionalization of a differentiated polity; during the nineteenth century, the Delaware and Iroquois did not form unified and differentiated political orders.

After 1907 only Alaska resembles a relatively free political environment for Native Americans, but again only the southeastern Alaska native communities formed ANB, while the other Alaskan groups—the Eskimos, the Aleuts, and the Athapascans—did not adopt centralized or differentiated forms of government. During the 1960s, under direct threat to the subsistence economy and land, Alaska's native groups organized AFN and lobbied for ANCSA. Since 1966 AFN has operated as an interest group for the collective goals of Alaska's indigenous groups, all of which perceive their condition as one unit. Nevertheless, one of the conditions for the formation and continuity of AFN has been the relatively pluralistic and administratively deregulated political environment in Alaska.

Despite the general absence of conditions that favor sustained collective action or institutional change in the lower 48, American Indian societies have shown strong cultural persistence. Traditional world views and associated commitments to nondifferentiated and decentralized social and political orders tend to inhibit the possibilities of institutional change and sustained collective action, but they are nonetheless a primary means by which many American Indian societies have resisted cultural and national annihilation. Societies with collective religious orientations were capable of mobilizing community action for protecting cultural and political interests, but were resistant to adopting institutions of increased political differentiation. The more socially and political solidary societies showed the most capacity for consensually adopting more centralized and differentiated governments, in response to threats to territory and political autonomy. In Alaska, which has self-governing villages, corporations, AFN organization, and resources from ANCSA—combined with a relative absence of American administrative regulation—there continue to be prospects for sustained collective action and institution building as a means to ensure political and cultural survival.

References

Adair, J.
  1775   *History of the American Indians*. London: Edward and Charles
             Dilly.
  1930   *Adair's History of the American Indians*. S. Williams, ed. Johnson
             City, TN: Watauga Press.

Akwesasne Notes, ed.
  1978   *Basic Call to Consciousness*. New York: Mohawk Nation.
  1980   The New Indian Elite: Bureaucratic Entrepreneurship. *Akwesasne
             Notes* (spring):18–19, 35.

The Alaska Fisherman
  1980   *The Alaska Fisherman: Special Edition*. Juneau, AK: Tlingit-Haida
             Central Council.

Alexander, J. C. and P. Colomy
  1985   Toward Neofunctionalism. *Sociological Theory* 3(2):11–23.

ANRC (Alaska Native Review Commission) (Volume No.)
  1984   *Alaska Native Review Commission Proceedings*. 50 vols. Mi-
             crofiche. Anchorage: Inuit Circumpolar Conference. (Available
             from Alaska State Library, Micrographics Production Lab, Pouch
             G, Juneau, AK 99811.)

Arnold, R. D.
  1978   *Alaska Native Land Claims*. Anchorage: Alaska Native Foundation.

Averkieva, J.
  1971   The Tlingit Indians. In Eleanor Leacock and Nancy Lurie, eds. *North
             American Indians in Historical Perspectives*. New York: Random
             House.

Baird, W. D.
  1972   *Peter Pitchlynn: Chief of the Choctaws*. Norman: University of
             Oklahoma Press.
  1974   *The Chickasaw People*. Phoenix, AZ: Indian Tribal Series.

1979   Peter Pitchlynn and the Reconstruction of the Choctaw Republic. In H. G. Jordan and T. Holm, eds. *Indian Leaders: Oklahoma's First Statesmen.* pp. 12–28. Oklahoma City: Oklahoma Historical Society.

Barden, G. B.
1953   The Colberts and the Chickasaw Nation. *The Tennessee Historical Quarterly* 17:22–249, 318–335.

Beck, P. V. and A. L. Walters
1977   *The Sacred: Ways of Knowledge Sources of Life.* Tsaile, AZ: Navajo Community College Press.

Bee, R. L.
1963   Changes in Yuma Social Organization. *Ethnology* 2:207–227.

1981   *Crosscurrents Along the Colorado: The Impact of Government Policy on the Quechan Indians.* Tucson: University of Arizona Press.

Berger, T. R.
1985   *Village Journey: The Report of the Alaska Native Review Commission.* New York: Hill and Wang.

Berkhofer, R. L., Jr.
1965   Faith and Factionalism Among the Senecas: Theory and Ethnohistory. *Ethnohistory* 12:99–112.

1977   *Salvation and the Savage.* Westport, CT: Greenwood Press.

Berry, M. C.
1975   *The Alaska Pipeline: The Politics of Oil and Native Land Claims.* Bloomington: Indiana University Press.

Billman, E., ed.
1969   A Potlatch Feast at Sitka, Alaska. *Anthropological Papers of the University of Alaska* 14:55–64.

Bird, M.
1983   The Effects of "Reagonomics" on the Northern Cheyenne Reservation: Preliminary Report. Lame Deer, MT. Mimeo.

Boggs, J.
1984   The Challenge of Reservation Resource Development: A Northern Cheyenne Instance. In J. Jorgensen, ed. *Native Americans and Economic Development.* pp. 205–236. Boston: Anthropology Resource Center.

Bourne, E. G., ed.
1922   *Narratives of the Career of Hernando de Soto.* 2 vols. New York: Allerton.

Brodeur, P.
1985   *Restitution: The Land Claims of the Mashpee, Passamaquoddy, and Penobscot Indians of New England.* Boston: Northeastern University Press.

Brown, J. P.
1938   *Old Frontiers.* Kingsport, TN: Southern Publishers.

Campbell, J.
1976a   *Occidental Mythology.* New York: Penguin Books.

| 1976b | *Primitive Mythology.* New York: Penguin Books. |

| 1988 | *Mythologies of the Great Hunt.* New York: Harper and Row. |

Carse, M. P.
1949   The Mohawk Iroquois. *Bulletin of the Archaeological Society of Connecticut* 23:3–53.

Castile, G.
1974   Federal Indian Policy and Sustained Enclave: An Anthropological Perspective. *Human Organization* 22:219–227.

Champagne, D.
1983a   Organizational Change and Conflict: A Case Study of the Bureau of Indian Affairs. *American Indian Culture and Research Journal* 7(3):3–28.

1983b   Symbolic Structure and Political Change in Cherokee Society. *Journal of Cherokee Studies* 8:87–96.

1983c   Social Structure, Revitalization Movements and State Building: Social Change in Four Native American Societies. *American Sociological Review* 48:754–763.

1985   Cherokee Social Movements: A Response to Thornton. *American Sociological Review* 50:127–130.

1988   The Delaware Revitalization Movement of the Early 1760s: A Suggested Reinterpretation. *The American Indian Quarterly* 2:107–126.

1989   Culture, Differentiation and Environment: Social Change in Tlingit Society. In J. C. Alexander and P. Colomy, eds. *Differentiation and Social Change: Historical and Comparative Perspectives.* Chapter 3. New York: Columbia University Press.

Chestnut, S.
1978   Coal Development on the Cheyenne Reservation. In *Proceedings of the U. S. Civil Rights Commission. Development in the Intermountain West: Its Impact on Women and Minorities.* Washington, DC: US Government Printing Office.

Cochran, T. C., ed.
1972   *The New American State Papers 1789–1860.* Vol. 1–13. Wilmington, DE: Scholarly Resources, Inc.

Corkran, D. H.
1957   Cherokee Pre-History. *The North Carolina Historical Review* 34:455–466.

1962   *The Creek Frontier 1540–1783.* Norman: University of Oklahoma Press.

1970   *The Carolina Indian Frontier.* Columbia, SC: University of South Carolina Press.

Cornell, S.
1984   Crisis and Response in Indian-White Relations, 1960–1984. *Social Problems* 32(1):44–59.

1988   *The Return of the Native: American Indian Political Resurgence.* New York: Oxford University Press.

Cotterill, B. S.
1954   *The Southern Indians: The Story of the Civilized Tribes Before
             Removal.* Norman: University of Oklahoma Press.

Croghan, G.
1916   George Croghan's Journal, Feb. 28, 1765–Oct. 8, 1765. In C.
             W. Alford and C. E. Carter, eds. *The New Regime, 1765–1767.*
             Collections of the Illinois State Historical Society, vol. XI.

Crow Impact Study Office
1977   A Social, Economic and Cultural Study of the Crow Reservation:
             Implications for Energy Development. Crow Tribe.

Debo, A.
1972   *The Rise and Fall of the Choctaw Republic.* Norman: University of
             Oklahoma Press.
1979   *The Road to Disappearance: A History of the Creek Indians.*
             Norman: University of Oklahoma Press.

de Laguna, F.
1954   Tlingit Ideas About the Individual. *Southwestern Journal of
             Anthropology* 10:172–191.

DeMallie, R. J.
1978   Pine Ridge Economy: Cultural and Historical Perspectives. In S.
             Stanley, ed. *American Indian Economic Development.* The Hague:
             Mouton.

Dickson, J. L.
1964   *The Judiciary History of the Cherokee Nation From 1721 to 1835.*
             Unpublished Ph.D. diss. University of Oklahoma, Norman.

Donaldson, T., ed.
1892   *Extra Census Bulletin. Indians, The Six Nations of New York.*
             Washington, DC: US Census Printing Office.

Drucker, P.
1939   Rank, Wealth, and Kinship in the Northwest Coast Society.
             American Anthropologist 41:55–65.
1958   The Native Brotherhoods: Modern Intertribal Organization on the
             Northwest Coast. *Bureau of American Ethnology Bulletin 168.*
             Washington, DC: US Government Printing Office.
1965   *Cultures of the North Pacific Coast.* San Francisco: Chandler.

Durkheim, E.
1984   *The Division of Labor in Society.* New York: Free Press.

Eaton, J. H.
1830   The Progress Made in Civilizing the Indians for the Last Eight Years
             and Their Present Condition. In *Report From the Secretary of War.*
             21st Congress, First Session, Vol. 2. pp. 110(1–22).

Edmunds, R. D.
1983   *The Shawnee Prophet.* Lincoln: University of Nebraska Press.

Edwards, J.
1983   The Choctaw Nation in the Middle of the Nineteenth Century. *The
             Chronicles of Oklahoma* 10:392–425.

Eisenstadt, S. N.

1964 Institutionalization and Social Change. *American Sociological Journal* 29:235-247.

1967 Transformation of Social, Political and Cultural Orders in Modernization. In R. Cohen and J. Middleton, eds. *Comparative Political Systems.* pp. 439-462. Austin: University of Texas Press.

1978 *Revolution and the Transformation of Societies.* New York: Free Press.

Engels, F.

1972 *The Origin of the Family, Private Property and the State.* New York: International Publishers.

Erdoes, R. and A. Ortiz, eds.

1984 *American Indian Myths and Legends.* New York: Pantheon Books.

Fenton, W. N.

1951 Locality as a Basic Factor in the Development of Iroquois Social Structure. In William Fenton, ed. *Bureau of Ethnology Bulletin 149.* Washington DC: US Government Printing Office.

1956 Toward the Gradual Civilization of the Indian Natives: The Missionary and Linguistic Work of Asher Wright (1803-1875) Among the Senecas of Western New York. *Proceedings of the American Philosophical Society* 100(6):567-581.

1957 Seneca Indians by Asher Wright (1859). *Ethnohistory* 4(3):304-321.

Ferguson, R. J.

1972 *The White River Delaware: An Ethnohistoric Synthesis 1795-1867.* Unpublished Ed.D. diss. Ball State University, Muncie, IN.

Foreman, C. T.

1966 *Indian Women Chiefs.* Norman: University of Oklahoma Press.

Fowler, L.

1982a *Arapahoe Politics, 1851-1978: Symbols in Crises of Authority.* Lincoln: University of Nebraska Press.

1982b "Look at My Hair, It Is Gray": Age Grading, Ritual Authority, and Political Change Among the Northern Arapahoe and Gros Ventre. In D. Ubelaker and H. Viola, eds. *Plains Indian Studies: A Collection of Essays in Honor of John C. Ewers and Waldo R. Wedel.* Washington, DC: Smithsonian Press.

1987 *Shared Symbols, Contested Meanings: Gros Ventre Culture and History, 1778-1984.* Ithaca, NY: Cornell University Press.

Frey, R.

1987 *The World of the Crow Indians: As Driftwood Lodges.* Norman: University of Oklahoma Press.

Fried, M.

1971 *The Notion of Tribe.* Menlo Park, CA: Cummings.

Garbarino, M.

1980 Independence and Dependency Among the Seminole of Florida. In E. L. Schusky, ed. *Political Organization of Native North Americans.* pp. 141-162. Washington, DC: University Press of America.

Gearing, F.
1962   Priests and Warriors: Social Structures for Cherokee Politics in the
                18th Century. *American Anthropologist.* Memoir 93. 64(5):1–124.

Gibson, A.
1971   *The Chickasaw.* Norman: University of Oklahoma Press.

Gilbert, W. H.
1943   The Eastern Cherokee. *Bureau of American Ethnology Bulletin 133.*
                Washington, DC: US Government Printing Office.

Gipson, L., ed.
1938   *Moravian Mission on White River.* Indianapolis: Indiana Historical
                Bureau.

Grant, C. L., ed.
1980   *Letters, Journals and Writings of Benjamin Hawkins.* Vol. 1, 1796–
                1801. Vol. 2, 1802–1816. Savannah, GA: Belview Press.

Graymont, B.
1972   *The Iroquois in the American Revolution.* Syracuse, NY: Syracuse,
                University Press.

Green, M. D.
1982   *The Politics of Indian Removal: Creek Government and Society in
                Crisis.* Lincoln: University of Nebraska Press.

Habermas, J.
1981   *Reason and the Rationalization of Society.* Vol. 1 of *The Theory of
                Communicative Action.* Trans. Thomas McCarthy. Boston: Beacon
                Press.

Hall, T. D.
1989   *Social Change in the Southwest, 1350–1880.* Lawrence: University
                Press of Kansas.

Hauptman, L.
1981   *The Iroquois and the New Deal.* Syracuse, NY: Syracuse University
                Press.

1986   *The Iroquois Struggle for Survival: World War II to Red Power.*
                Syracuse, NY: Syracuse University Press.

Hawkins, B.
1916   *Letters of Benjamin Hawkins 1796–1806.* Collection of the Georgia
                Historical Society, Vol. 9. Savannah: Georgia Historical Society.

Hazard, S., ed.
1851–52   *Pennsylvania Colonial Records.* Vol. 5, 1745–1754. Philadelphia:
                State of Pennsylvania.

Heckewelder, J.
1876   *History, Manners, and Customs of the Indian Nations.* Philadelphia:
                The Historical Society of Pennsylvania.

Hendrix, J. B.
1983   Redbird Smith and the Nighthawk Keetoowahs. *Journal of Cherokee
                Studies* 8:73–86.

Henri, F.
1986   *The Southern Indians and Benjamin Hawkins 1796–1816.* Norman:
                University of Oklahoma Press.

Herring, J. B.
1988   *Kenekuk: The Kickapoo Prophet.* Lawrence: The University Press of Kansas.

Hertzberg, H. W.
1971   *The Search for an American Indian Identity.* Syracuse, NY: Syracuse University Press.

Hewitt, J. N.
1939   Notes on the Creek Indians. In J. R. Swanton, ed. *Bureau of American Ethnology Bulletin 123.* Washington, DC: US Government Printing Office.

Hoebel, E. A.
1978   *The Cheyennes: Indians of the Great Plains.* New York: Holt, Rinehart and Winston.

Hope, A., III
1975   *Founders of the Alaska Native Brotherhood.* Sitka, AK: Special Edition.

Hudson, P. J.
1939   A Story of Choctaw Chiefs. *The Chronicles of Oklahoma* 17:7-16, 192-211.

Hultkrantz, A.
1979   *The Religions of the American Indians.* Berkeley: University of California Press.

IPH (Volume No.)
1937   *Indian Pioneer History Collection.* 122 vols. Grant Foreman, ed. Microfilm. Oklahoma City: Oklahoma Historical Society.

Iverson, P.
1981   *The Navajo Nation.* Westport, CT: Greenwood Press.

Jorgensen, J.
1972   *The Sun Dance Religion.* Chicago: University of Chicago Press.

Jorgensen, J., ed.
1986   Special Issue: American Indian Governments in the Reagan Era. *American Indian Culture and Research Journal* 10(2):1-94.

Josephy, A. M., Jr.
1984   *Now That the Buffalo's Gone: A Study of Today's American Indians.* Norman: University of Oklahoma Press.

Kelly, L.
1986   The Indian Reorganization Act: The Dream and the Reality. In R. L. Nichols, ed. *The American Indian Past and Present.* New York: Alfred A. Knopf.

Kenny, J.
1913   Journal of James Kenny, 1761-1763. *The Pennsylvania Magazine of History and Biography* 37:1-47, 152-201.

King, D., ed.
1979   *The Cherokee Indian Nation: A Troubled History.* Knoxville: University of Tennessee Press.

Klien, L.
1980   Contending With Colonization: Tlingit Men and Women in Change. In M. Etienne and E. Leacock, eds. *Women and Colonization.* New York: Praeger.

Knight, O.
1953   Fifty Years of Choctaw Law, 1834–1884. *The Chronicles of Oklahoma* 31:76–95.

Kraft, H. C.
1986   *The Lenape: Archeology, History, and Ethnography.* Newark: New Jersey Historical Society.

Krause, A.
1956   *The Tlingit Indians.* Seattle: American Ethnological Society.

Lamphere, L.
1977   *To Run After Them.* Tucson: University of Arizona Press.

Leder, L. H, ed.
1956   *The Livingstone Indian Records 1666–1723.* Gettysburg: The Pennsylvania Historical Association.

Lewis, J. R.
1988   Shamans and Prophets: Continuities and Discontinuities in Native American Religions. *The American Indian Quarterly* 12(3):221–228.

Liberty, M.
1965   Suppression and Survival of the Northern Cheyenne Sun Dance. *Minnesota Archeologist* 27:120–143.

Lincecum, G., comp.
1861   *Traditional History of the Chahta Nation.* Microfilmed ms. Austin: University of Texas Library, Eugene C. Barker Texas History Center.

Longe, A.
1969   A Small Postscript on the Ways and Manners of the Indians Called Cherokee. David Corkran, ed. *Southern Indian Studies* 21:10–16.

Lowie, R. H.
1956   *The Crow Indians.* New York: Holt, Rinehart and Winston.

1967   Some Aspects of Political Organization Among the American Aborigines. In R. Cohen and J. Middleton, eds. *Comparative Political Systems.* pp. 63–87. Austin: University of Texas Press.

M234
nd   *Letters Received by the Office of Indian Affairs 1824–1881.* Bureau of Indian Affairs Record Group 75. Microfilm. Washington, DC: National Archives.

McBeath, G. and T. A. Morehouse
1980   *The Dynamics of Alaska Native Self-Government.* Washington, DC: University Press of America.

McLoughlin, W. G.
1984   *The Cherokee Ghost Dance.* Mercer, GA: Mercer University Press.

Metcalfe, P. M.
1985   *The Central Council 50 Years: Commemorating the Jurisdictional Act of June 19, 1935.* Juneau: The Central Council of the Tlingit & Haida Indian Tribes of Alaska.

MH (*Missionary Herald*)
1805-89   *The Missionary Herald.* Vols. 1-85. Cambridge, MA: The Harvard Divinity School Library.

Miles, G.
1976   A Brief Study of Joseph Brant's Political Career in Relation to Iroquois Political Structure. *American Indian Journal* 2(12):12-20.

Morgan, L. H.
1959   *The Indian Journals 1859-1862.* Ann Arbor: University of Michigan Press.

1977   *Ancient Society.* New York: Gorder.

Nairne, T.
1988   *Nairnes' Muskhogean Journals: The 1708 Expedition to the Mississippi River.* A. Moore, ed. Jackson: University Press of Mississippi.

Newcomb, W. W., Jr.
1956   *The Culture and Acculturation of the Delaware Indians.* Ann Arbor: University of Michigan Museum of Anthropology.

NCTR
1983   Northern Cheyenne Tribal Records. Lame Deer, MT: Northern Cheyenne Research Project.

Nordstrom, J., J. Boggs, N. J. Owen and J. Sooktis
1977   *The Northern Cheyenne Tribe and Energy Development in South Eastern Montana. Volume 1: Social, Cultural and Economic Investigations.* Billings, MT: Old West Regional Commission.

Norton, J.
1970   *Journal of Major John Norton.* C. Klinck and J. Talman, eds. Toronto: Champlain Society.

Oberg, K.
1960   Kinship Sentiment and the Structure of Social Action. In W. Goldschmidt, ed. *Exploring the Ways of Mankind.* pp. 290-295. New York: Holt, Rinehart and Winston.

1973   *The Social Economy of the Tlingit Indians.* Seattle: University of Washington Press.

Ohland, M.
1930   The Government of the Creek Indians. *The Chronicles of Oklahoma* 8:42-64, 189-225.

Olsen, R. L.
1967   Social Structure and Social Life of the Tlingit in Alaska. *Anthropological Records Vol. 26.* Berkeley: University of California Press.

Owens, N. and J. P. Boggs
1977   The Reservation in the Regional Economy. Lame Deer, MT: Northern Cheyenne Research Project.

Owens, N. and K. Peres
1980   Overcoming Institutional Barriers to Economic Development on the Northern Cheyenne Reservation. Lame Deer, MT: Northern Cheyenne Research Project.

The Panopolist
1806–07   *The Panopolist* Volume 1. (Later *The Missionary Herald;* see MH).

Parsons, T.
1977   *The Evolution of Societies.* Englewood Cliffs, NJ: Prentice-Hall.

Payne, J.
nd   *John Payne Papers.* 14 vols. Microfilm. Chicago: Newberry Library.

PCIRE (Presidential Commission on Indian Reservation Economies)
1984   *Report and Recommendations to the President of the United States.* Washington, DC: US Government Printing Office.

Perdue, T.
1979   *Slavery and the Evolution of Cherokee Society 1540–1866.* Knoxville: University of Tennessee Press.

Powell, P.
1969   *Sweet Medicine.* 2 vols. Norman: University of Oklahoma Press.

1980   *The Cheyenne, Ma?heo?o's People: A Critical Bibliography.* Bloomington: Indiana University Press.

1981   *People of the Sacred Mountain: A History of the Northern Cheyenne Chiefs and Warrior Societies 1830–1879, with an Epilogue 1969–1874.* 2 vols. San Francisco: Harper and Row.

Powers, W. K.
1977   *Oglala Sioux.* Lincoln: University of Nebraska Press.

Pringle, R. M.
1958   *The Northern Cheyenne Indians in the Reservation Period.* B.A. honors thesis. Harvard University, Cambridge, MA.

Ritzenthaler, R. E.
1950   The Oneida Indians in Wisconsin. *Bulletin of the Public Museum of the City of Milwaukee* 19:1–58.

Rogers, G. W.
1960   *Alaska in Transition.* Baltimore: Johns Hopkins University Press.

Roll, T. E.
1979   Crow Chieftainships: A Study of Status Acquisition. *Occasional Papers of the Museum of the Rockies* 1:99–108.

Rosman, A. and P. Rubel
1972   The Potlatch: A Structural Analysis. *American Anthropologist* 74:658–671.

Rowland, D.
1907   *Encyclopedia of Mississippi History.* Vol. 1. Madison, WI: S. A. Brant.

Rowland, D., ed.
1911   *Mississippi Provincial Archives 1763–1766.* Vol. 1. Nashville: Press of Brandon Printing Co.

Rowland, D. and A. G. Sanders, eds.
1927   *Mississippi Provincial Archives 1729–1740.* Vol. 1. Jackson: Press of Mississippi Department of Archives and History.

1932   *Mississippi Provincial Archives 1704–1743.* Vol. 3. Jackson: Press of Mississippi Department of Archives and History.

Sahlins, M. D.
1968   *Tribesmen.* Englewood Cliffs, NJ: Prentice-Hall.

Salisbury, O.
1962   *Quoth the Raven: A Little Journey into the Primitive.* Seattle: Superior.

Schusky, E. L.
1975   *The Forgotten Sioux: An Ethnohistory of the Lower Brule Reservation.* Chicago: Nelson-Hall.

Sequin, M.
1985   Interpretative Contexts for Traditional and Current Coast Tsimshian Feasts. *Canadian Ethnology Service Paper No. 98.* Ottawa: National Museum of Man.

Shepardson, M.
1963   *Navajo Ways in Government: A Study in Political Process. American Anthropologist.* Memoir 96. 65(3).

1965   Problems of the Navajo Tribal Courts in Transition. *Human Organization* 24:250–53.

Skocpol, T.
1979   *States and Social Revolutions.* New York: Cambridge University Press.

Smelser, N. J.
1973   Toward a Theory of Modernization. In A. Etzioni and E. Etzioni-Halevy, eds. *Social Change: Sources, Patterns and Consequences.* pp. 268–284. New York: Basic Books.

1985   Evaluating the Model of Structural Differentiation in Relation to Educational Change in the Nineteenth Century. In J. C. Alexander, ed. *Neofunctionalism.* pp. 113–130. Beverly Hills, CA: Sage.

Smith, C.
1982   Planning Development Impacts on Indian Reservations. In C. Geiser, ed. *Indian SIA: The Social Impact Assessment of Rapid Resource Development on Native Peoples.* pp. 41–55. University of Michigan: Natural Resource Sociology Lab.

Spicer, E. H.
1962   *Cycles of Conquest.* Tucson: University of Arizona Press.

Steacy, S.
1971   The Chickasaw Nation on the Eve of the Civil War. *The Chronicles of Oklahoma.* 49:51–74.

Stevenson, I.
1966   Seven Cases Suggestive of Reincarnation Among the Tlingit Indians of Southeastern Alaska. *Proceedings of the American Society for Psychical Research* 26:191–240.

Straus, A.
1978   The Meaning of Death in Northern Cheyenne Culture. *Plains Anthropologist* 23:1–16.

Swanton, J. R.
1908   Social Organization, Beliefs and Linguistic Relationship of the Tlingit Indians. *Twenty-sixth Annual Report of the U. S. Bureau of American Ethnology, 1904-05.* Washington, DC: US Government Printing Office.

1915   The Social Significance of the Creek Confederacy. *Proceedings of the International Congress of Americanists* 19:327-334.

1928   Social Organization and Social Usages of the Creek Confederacy. *Forty-Second Annual Report of the United States Bureau of American Ethnology.* pp. 25-472. Washington, DC: US Government Printing Office.

Taylor, T.
1984   *The Bureau of Indian Affairs.* Boulder, CO: Westview Press.

Tilly, C.
1978   *From Mobilization to Revolution.* Reading, MA: Addison-Wesley.

Tolkein, B.
1969   The Pretty Languages of Yellowman. *Genre* 3:211-235.

Tollefson, K.
1977   A Structural Change in Tlingit Potlatching. *Western Canadian Journal of Anthropology* 7:16-24.

1978   From Local Clans to Regional Corporations: The Acculturation of the Tlingit. *Western Canadian Journal of Anthropology* 8:1-20.

Trafzer, C. E. and M. A. Beach
1986   Smohalla, The Washani, and Religion as a Factor in Northwestern Indian History. In C. E. Trafzer, ed. *American Indian Prophets.* pp. 71-86. Sacramento, CA: Sierra Oaks Publishing Company.

Tucker, N.
1969   Nancy Ward, Ghighau of the Cherokees. *The Georgia Historical Quarterly* 53(2):1,969.

Voget, F.
1952   Crow Socio Cultural Groups. In S. Tax, ed. *Acculturation in the Americas. Proceedings and Selected Papers of the XXIXth International Congress of Americanists.* Vol. II.

1980   Adaptation and Cultural Persistence Among the Crow Indians of Montana. In E. L. Schusky, ed. *Political Organization of Native North Americans.* pp. 163-188. Washington DC: University Press of America.

Wallace, A. F. C.
1956   New Religions Among the Delaware Indians, 1600-1900. *Southwestern Journal of Anthropology* 12:18-19.

1972   *The Death and Rebirth of the Seneca.* New York: Vintage Books.

Wallerstein, I.
1984   *The Politics of the World-Economy: The States, the Movements and the Civilizations.* New York: Cambridge University Press.

Wahrhaftig, A. and J. Luken-Wahrhaftig
1979   New Militants or Resurrected State? The Five County Northeastern Oklahoma Cherokee Organization. In D. King, ed. *The Cherokee Indian Nation: A Troubled History.* pp. 223–246. Knoxville: University of Tennessee Press.

Weber, M.
1963   *The Sociology of Religion.* Boston: Beacon Press.

Weist, K.
1973   Give Away: The Ceremonial Distribution of Goods Among the Northern Cheyenne of Southeastern Montana. *Plains Anthropologist* 18:97–103.

Weist, T.
1977   *A History of the Cheyenne People.* Billings, MT: Council for Indian Education.

Weslager, C. A.
1972   *The Delaware Indians.* New Brunswick, NJ: Rutgers University Press.
1978   *The Delaware Indian Westward Migration.* Wallingford, PA: Middle Atlantic Press.

Whiteman, H. V.
1973   Paper read before the American Studies Convention, 20 October 1973. Lame Deer, MT: Northern Cheyenne Tribal Records.

Wilkins, T.
1986   *Cherokee Tragedy: The Ridge Family and the Decimation of a People.* Norman: University of Oklahoma Press.

Williams, A.
1970   Navajo Political Process. *Smithsonian Contributions to Anthropology.* Vol. 9. Washington DC: Smithsonian Institution Press.

Wilson, E.
1959   *Apologies to the Iroquois.* New York: Farrar, Straus and Cudahy.

Wolf, E.
1969   *Peasant Wars of the Twentieth Century.* New York: Harper and Row.

Woodenlegs
1979   The Cheyenne Way of Life. *Occasional Papers of the Museum of the Rockies* 1:57–61.

Wyatt, V.
1984   *History of Relations Between Indians and Caucasians in Southeast Alaska.* Unpublished Ph.D. diss. Yale University, New Haven, CT.

Young, M. E.
1961   *Redskins, Ruffleshirts and Rednecks: Indian Allotments in Alabama and Mississippi, 1830–1860.* Norman: University of Oklahoma Press.

Young, R. W.
1978   *A Political History of the Navajo Tribe.* Tsaile, AZ: Navajo Community College Press.

Zeisberger, D.
1910   *David Zeisberger's History of the North American Indians.* A. Hulbert and W. Scwarze, eds. Ohio State Archaeological and Historical Society.